Marianne invites us all into her stor̲   ...... I ....
Imagine yourself in her story. Think about what she learned, about what is still learning, about what we can learn. It reminded me of my own pain. That is life, isn't it? Life includes many disappointments, many stories. But her story also includes hope. You will find all of those elements in this book. Open the pages. Open your mind. Open your heart. Welcome to the journey.

— Chris Maxwell - Author, Speaker, Spiritual Director

Written from the heart, this book inspires a new awakening and growing faith in the Almighty as you prepare your home and heart for motherhood.

— Susan Friedmann - CSP, international bestselling author of Riches in Niches: How to Make It Big in a Small Market

A true testament to God's grace and redemptive power. Written in a down-to-earth and relatable voice, Petersen takes the reader back thirty years to when she was a new Christian trying to figure out what God would have her do in her difficult situation. Her story is sure to resonate with other young women who are facing unexpected pregnancies, and show how God will be with them and guide them as well.

— Jay Hobbs - Editor, Pregnancy Help News

I read God and My Pillow in one sitting. With humor and honesty the story holds you to the unexpected ending. What a witness Marianne is for allowing God to lead her in a time of uncertainty that applies to all lives, pregnant or not.

— Wendy - Amazon Customer

Marianne has a witty sense of humor, but also gives a very raw and honest account of how she navigated through the struggles and questions that emerge through pregnancy, and as a new mom. Whether you're experiencing an unplanned pregnancy, or simply want a reminder of how faithful God is, this is a wonderful book filled with hope!

— Trina Wilson - wife, mother of four

This book is perfect for the young woman who has found herself in the same predicament as the author, and it can act as a forewarning to any young girl. Reading "God and My Pillow" encouraged me to face my own reality of my own unique challenges, and take responsibility knowing that I can trust Jesus all the way.

— Willma Redhed, wife, mother of two, art instructor

God and My Pillow

Learning to Trust Through the Unexpected

- A MEMOIR -

Marianne Petersen

A true smile it
brings to me giving
this book to you !
Love
Marianne

God and My Pillow -
Learning to Trust Through the Unexpected

Copyright © 2018

ISBN 978-0-578-60182-3

All scripture quotations are taken from the Holy Bible, New King James Version ®. Copyright © 1994 by Thomas Nelson, Inc.

Any internet addresses in this book are offered as a resource.
They are not intended in any way to imply an endorsement to or from them.

Cover design - Lynnette Bonner at indiecoverdesign.com
Interior design and typeset - Jon Stewart at stewartdesign.studio
Editing - Sheryl Madden at sheryl-madden.com

All photos courtesy of the author - Printed in the United States of America

To two very special people

Michelle Novak - the one I happily blame for getting me to write this book.

Cassie MacHale - as you read, you will find out why.

And of course to God . . . and my pillow.

Author's Note

A few names have been changed, and, of course, the exact wording of every conversation that took place could not be remembered perfectly. (But darn near close.)

God and My Pillow is not just to help those dealing with an unplanned pregnancy, but to also encourage all women to follow that one well-known saying: wait for your wedding night.

Oh, and also for those who just need a good, old-fashioned love story.

Contents

INTRODUCTION

Years ago, my pillow began its toughest job: listening to all my thoughts that were consumed with guilt, embarrassment, questions, worry, shame, and regret. Only my pillow knew my deepest wish, that I would wake up to discover being pregnant was not real but just a dream.

Later, people encouraged me to write about this soap opera I experienced. I couldn't help but want to call this book My Pillow, since my pillow was the one thing that knew all my thoughts during that time.

Wait! I thought as I got deeper into writing. How dare I not include who else knew all my thoughts: God! He knew far more than anyone or anything else. My Pillow instantly changed to God and My Pillow. Perfect.

I pray my experience helps you cope with this same type of trial or any other life-changing ordeals God and your pillow know about. I hope it helps put the pieces of your life back together while showing that, if your heart is turned toward God, everything falls into place.

CHAPTER 1
That Unfinished Fourth-of-July Thought

"Okay, who's ready for the fireworks?" one of my three older brothers asked as everyone was waiting for the sun to go down. A fun-filled, family-and-friends Fourth of July, indeed. One of the most enjoyable, relaxing times I'd had in months. My mom made sure our dinner was perfect. Sort of her way to say how happy she was I had come back home just a few days earlier from a three-month stay in California. Dad sure was thrilled to once again call me Winnipoops in person and not just over the phone. Crazy nickname, I know.

"You all better be careful," Mom joyously demanded while bringing out a few folding chairs in case anyone wanted to sit down in the front yard. Two of my three older sisters were also there. Yes, I'm the youngest of seven. And to top off this ideal setting, my best friend, Willma, was also there, partaking in all the fun.

Man, it feels good to be back home. I'm so thankful those three months in California are now history. I'll give it my all this next quarter when I get back to taking classes at Highline Community College. A fresh new start. Many peaceful thoughts went through my brain as I was soaking in the positive vibes all around me.

I had missed this house in Normandy Park, a small town south of Seattle. I missed the big front yard at the end of our dead-end street. I missed my bedroom that looked out over the front yard from my second-floor window. I missed the creek at the bottom of the hill in our big backyard. I certainly missed the fireplace in the living room. Heck, I even missed the TV room my siblings and I would fight in as to who got to choose the channel. What I mostly missed, however, was being around my family and friends. Yes, I certainly loved being back home.

That Fourth of July in 1986 started out great, but was definitely different from all the ones before and, as you'll soon read, all the ones after. As people were having a blast—literally—with fireworks, while standing and gazing up at the next firework I asked myself this one certain question. A question that changed my life.

I wonder why I haven't started my period? My thoughts continued. *Oh, it's probably just a few days late because of all these different emotions I've been feeling with moving back home. That's it. That driving-back adventure from California must be why. I just lost track of my cycle. Nothing else. Hmmm. But four days? That couldn't mean I might be preg...* That thought stopped halfway through the last word.

No, wait! I almost said PREGNANT! My heart began to pound a bit faster. My thoughts continued. *NO! This is my first time ever thinking that.* One daunting thought, indeed. That thought began to grow. No way could I stand up any longer. All of a sudden I was extremely glad my mom had brought out those chairs. I sat down. Not only was I thinking I might be pregnant, but also, that if I was, I'd then be stereotyped as someone who just doesn't know what she's doing and would get looked down upon by many.

I had to force myself not to show any signs of being worried as all the others were enjoying lighting fireworks. Everyone else was asking if they could light the next firework. Me? I was asking myself if I was just a few days late or if I was pregnant.

But I'm a Christian. I... I can't! Pregnant? Could I? No. Please, no. I... I can't be. It was my very first time. No way could I be pregnant from doing "it" only once!

Yep, being a Christian made me feel even worse with this possibility. Twenty-million questions were forming inside my head as I heard questions on the outside as well.

"Marianne, you want to light this firework?" I was occasionally asked.

"No, thanks. You guys are better at that. I'll just sit here and watch," while wishing I wasn't thinking about what I was thinking about.

"Really? Are you sure?"

"Yes. Thanks, though."

I'll never forget that evening: sitting on a folding chair, watching everyone have fun while I faked a grin for the remainder of the night. Even though I was surrounded by dear family and friends, those thoughts I was having made me feel totally alone. I began to realize how even God-fearing Christians could mess up, being that I was, at age nineteen, one of them. An instantaneous new perspective on life began that night. Not the fun, firework-filled Fourth I had expected, that's for sure.

Later, with my head on my pillow, I was miserable, wishing I could just stay still, go to sleep, and wake up from a nightmare. But instead, I was rolling over every few minutes. The thought was driving me crazy. I was shocked at myself for even allowing this possibility to exist. I was lying in bed, my pillow drowning from the overflow of worries.

No. I can't be thinking this. This shouldn't have come close to happening. These thoughts were soaking my pillow with fear. *I'm different! I'm a Christian now. I know what I did was wrong, and God heard my pleas for forgiveness. I can't be! I just can't. I'm back at home with Mom and Dad, and I have a great career plan. God, please don't have me be pregnant.*

What seemed like millions of those thoughts had me tossing and turning on my pillow, left and right, left and right. My pillow must have felt like screaming, "BE STILL, MARIANNE!"

No, no, don't wake up. I don't wanna open my eyes. The new day had started. My mind seemed to be as it was just a few hours before. I grew increasingly worried, increasingly anxious, increasingly, no pun intended, sick to my stomach.

I got up and just gave it my all, trying to ignore it in the hope I was wrong, and, for the first time ever, wishing I would start my period at any second. I looked at myself in the mirror a little differently as soon as I got out of bed. Guess what I looked at? Yep, my stomach.

No. I can't be. I just CANNOT be pregnant. I then looked at my face. Not too happy of a face, I might add. I also considered a bit more about my weight. I was, sad to say, already on the heavy side, so of course I thought I would be getting even heavier. Not good.

Stop thinking. Just go downstairs. And down I went. Most every morning I could go into the living room to find my mom sitting down on the floor in front of the fireplace, with a cigarette in hand, her coffee cup and the ashtray right next to her. No fire going, but that room was to her as my pillow on my bed was to me: a place to escape and just think while looking into the fireplace as if a fire were going.

"Hi, Mom," I said as I sat on the couch that directly faced the fireplace, three or so yards away, wishing there was a fire to distract me. "After I eat breakfast, I think I'll go hang out with Willma for a while. Anything you want me to do around here before I go?" My reason for asking that was totally selfish. I needed stuff to do to keep my mind busy.

"Thanks, Marianne. I'll let you know later. You can just go over to Willma's. That's fine."

Hours went by as I faked a grin while hanging out with Willma, the same fake grin I made up on the Fourth of July. No period. I avoided any type of deep talk about anything with anyone. I tried my hardest to get it off my mind. I actually did, for a minute here and there anyway, forcing the thought that it's perfectly normal to occasionally start a day or two... or four late.

Somehow I managed to get to sleep that night. Knowing I'd be going to church the next morning helped. Going to Emmanuel Baptist Church since being home was great, and doing so helped me think of more positive things than about that other thing that consumed my thoughts.

Oh, what a blessing it was to see those familiar faces again and get back to solid truth being taught. First time in months.

"So nice seeing you again. What brought you back?" many asked.

I gave the many reasons I did have that were all legit, but no way could I say my main reason: to escape. *Start, period, start. Please. PLEASE start!*

That Sunday night, face down on my pillow, I decided that if I hadn't started by that next morning, I'd find a place to get a pregnancy test. Marianne Ignorant Houstoun I was in how to find one.

Let me explain my middle name. Being the youngest of seven and not having been given a middle name, I grew up thinking of a fun reason why: they must have run out of ideas by the time I came along. I still have fun making up my middle name to go with whatever mood I'm in. And thinking for the first time on how to find out if I was pregnant, ignorant I sure was. I rolled onto my back, staring at the ceiling, planning what I'd do that next morning. I figured it out. *As soon as Dad goes to work and Mom's not anywhere near the phone book, I'll grab it and find a place to go for a test. I have to.*

CHAPTER 2

Positive Sure Seemed Negative

The new day had arrived. Nope, I didn't start. I walked down the stairs finding out Dad was gone and Mom was by the fireplace. No cordless phones back then, and I didn't dare use the kitchen phone, saying for the world to hear, "Hello. Can I come in and get a pregnancy test?" even if I was the only one home. I did have a phone in my room, but still, I felt better just waiting until my mom had to go somewhere.

As soon as she did, I grabbed those yellow pages in the kitchen that seemed to be staring at me, ran upstairs to my room, and shut the door. (Hey, you can't be too safe.) *Where to begin? Test? No, too generic. Pregnancy test? There, that should do it.*

During all the page flipping, it felt like I was a spy who was taking forever to find an important number. *I can't believe I'm doing this. I can't believe I'm doing this. I guess I'll look under 'Pregnancy Test.' Okay, let's see. Planned Parenthood. This sure wasn't planned, but I guess I have to plan something if I am.*

That was the first one I noticed. After all, that's what the bold wording is supposed to do, right? Make you notice. Well, it worked. I was so nervous pressing those numbers.

Ring, ring. Ring, ring. Ring, ring. Ring, ring.

Hmmm. No answer. Darn it. I'll try another one. I'll flip back a bit and go in alphabetical order. Let's see, Crisis Pregnancy Center. This sure is a crisis for me if I'm pregnant. I have to try this one.

Ring, ring. Ring, ring.

Oh, please. Oh, please be open! PLEASE be op...

"Hello. Crisis Pregnancy Center. How can I help you?"

Please tell me I'm not pregnant. "Just seeing if you are open today. Really? Right now? Thank you." Click.

No one was around, thankfully, so I just checked my face one last time, grabbed my purse, and took off. Swiftly walking to my car, my mom was getting out of hers.

"Where ya going?" she asked while pulling out a grocery bag. "I just went to Alber..."

"Hi, Mom. Sorry, gotta run."

"When will you be back?"

"Not sure. Bye."

God, help me. Please, please, help me. I couldn't decide if I wanted all the lights to be red and delay the test results for as long as possible or if I wanted them all green so I could just get it over with. Assuming it would be a normal doctor's office, I was surprised when all I pulled up to was just one door to a small building. *Oh, well. Whatever.*

Reality hit me right then and there as I put my car in park. I stayed in it for a few minutes. *Okay, I can do this. I still can't believe it. God, please help me, I can do this.* Out of the car I went, still thinking how that place sure didn't have that doctor's-office look. Marianne Dreading-To-Go-In Houstoun became my new name. As I opened the door, I noticed a tiny waiting area with a few simple pictures of beautiful landscapes on the walls, a few desks, and a few doors here and there. One door was partly open, and I took a glance inside. I noticed a large screen on the wall, but as I was looking in, I heard a voice.

"Hello. Can I help you?"

Oh. I'd best act sophisticated.

"Yes," I replied. "I was informed I can get a pregnancy test here. I would like to have one, please. I was also told the test is free, right?"

This one middle-aged lady was so nice. No uniform, like I had expected. She just wore nice but relaxed-looking shirt and slacks.

"Yes, it is. We can do one now after you fill out this form."

Thankfully it wasn't too long to fill out. *I can't believe I'm doing this. I can't believe I'm doing this.* Heck, I almost wrote that thought down on one long empty line, I was thinking it so much.

Only a minute or so after I turned it in, one of those doors opened with a different woman coming over to me.

Okay, here we go. I can't believe I'm doing this.

As I walked in, that woman, looking to be in her thirties, kindly welcomed me in, showing me where to sit.

"Hello, Marianne. I'm glad we can help you today. I know what you are here for, and I hope I can answer any questions you might have," she said warmly. "I do, however, have one question before we go any further. Do you have plans yet what you will do if the test shows you are pregnant?"

Wow. I realized right then and there that I never really thought about that. What *would* I do? So far I had only wondered if I am pregnant, but not really what if the *if* turned out to be *yes.*

After being asked that, I instantly thought about the goal I had made for my life, to be one who succeeded with an impressive career. My overall thought was that I was a Christian, and knowing my three sisters each had experienced an unplanned pregnancy, I didn't want to follow that path. But my main reason was that no way in the world did I want God to look bad by having one of His own children be a single, pregnant teenager.

"Well, there's no way I can have a baby when I'm so young." That made total sense to me the more I thought about it. "I believe that the best thing I should do is have an abortion. It's really nothing much inside me yet anyway, so I think it's fine for me to abort."

The lady was so kind in listening as I gave my ever-so-sophisticated answer. She did not, however, respond for or against.

"Well, before we talk about it much, let's do the test."

So, there I was in the bathroom. *I can't believe I'm doing this.* I held this little cup under myself as I sat on the toilet. Then back to the room, holding that most-important little cup filled with my future.

"Now, Marianne," she calmly said, "as I said before, we are not a doctor's office. That means we are not qualified to say what, for sure, this test says. We will show you how it's done and tell you what the color it shows says, but we cannot read the results to you." I was soaking in every word she said as she continued on. "Are you ready?"

"I think so," I said.

I was then given a small piece of what looked like candy, about the size of an M&M.

"Drop this in the cup and stir it a few times. If it turns reddish, it's positive. If it stays its original color, then it's negative," she said. "Ready?"

Ready as I'll ever be. I placed that little piece and stirred those few times. *I can't believe I'm doing this.* Man, was I scared. The mixing was done.

"Marianne, do you see what it's telling you?"

"Yes, yes, I do. I'm pretty sure, anyway." I saw it slowly changing to red, and with the biggest smile on my face, I said, "IT'S RED! And red means positive, and since positive means good, that means I'm not pregnant!" I felt so relieved. *Oh! AMEN!*

"Um, Marianne," she said in her calm voice, "for pregnancy tests, positive means pregnant."

Silence. My heart collapsed. *I must have misunderstood her.* "Did you say positive means I AM pregnant?" I didn't like my question. I more so didn't like her answer.

"Yes, the test shows you are pregnant."

More silence. I felt totally disconnected from everything around me as I looked down at the floor.

After a short spell she asked, "Is it okay if I ask you—now that this test shows you are pregnant—what you think you should do?"

I took a deep breath, feeling like I needed to be strong and not fall into a pit of despair.

"Yes, you can. I... I still think I should get an abortion. I can't be a bad example as a Christian. You may not understand what I mean by all that, but I want to please God and be a good witness to others."

I actually felt a little relaxed as I said that. Everyone had hopes for me, for my future, and I did too. I felt the troubles of having a baby and messing up all my plans would far outweigh the discomfort of getting an abortion. After all, I have to show the world I'm a God-fearing woman who can, with God's help, strive at my goals and do great in this world. V-I-C-T-O-R-Y! But also, I didn't want to turn out to be one of those single moms I assumed just lived off of Welfare.

This woman, very loving and accepting of me, shared how Crisis Pregnancy Center is a Christian organization. She opened my eyes to the facts I needed to know. Those facts? God is my Father, He loves me, and victory to Him is a bit different than my view of victory. She helped me put two and two together, showing me I needed to change my way of thinking and see God's thoughts on abortion. He did not want me to have an abortion. Those minutes opened my eyes to one precious fact: God wants me to have this baby. If I'm truly one of God's children, then I should be understanding and agree with what God says. She could tell I was young and uninformed on what God's word says about abortion, so she showed me right then and there, verse after verse, how God knew this baby was forming in me and that he or she was planned. God knew about this baby before it was even conceived.

After talking for a while, after my heart started feeling a bit of peace, she showed me a video on the screen in that one room I was curious about earlier.

"Marianne, have you ever seen a picture of what a six-week-old looks like inside someone's tummy?" she asked.

"No."

"This video shows what the different stages of pregnancy are like."

There on that screen I watched a video that confirmed what I was learning. Tears came to my eyes as I saw what this *thing* looked like in my tummy. It wasn't, to me, just a *thing* anymore. It was a real human being. I decided right then and there that there was no way in the world I could have an abortion. I felt like the biggest fool, thinking that aborting this baby, this real, living human, would keep me as a holier-than-thou example to everyone.

I thanked that woman so much for opening my eyes. She also informed me how the first place I called would most likely have encouraged me to abort this baby, promising it would be the right decision and a simple procedure. I felt right then that God wanted me to have that pregnancy test at Crisis Pregnancy Center, thus had planned to have that first phone call just ring and ring and ring.

When I had walked into that building, I had felt dread. Walking out, I felt peace. Thankfulness. The love of God surrounding me. That lady in that small building was the tool God used to show me He'd help me through this trial ahead. It was then that I felt His grace fall like rain on me, washing away my pain of worry. I learned in that little office how God's hand can guide my way, and I must walk by faith even when I cannot see what might be on the rough road ahead. *Thank you, God, for making sure no one answered that first phone call I made.*

It took me a while to start up the car as I just sat, thinking. I knew as soon as I left, I would have much in front of me, and I'm not talking about traffic and lights. I'm talking about the new life I was carrying, new decisions I needed to make, new things to be stressed over and worried about, and, of course, getting used to all the physical changes I'd be having with this baby growing inside. This new road ahead, however, had a great driver. No, not me. God, who had a perfect traffic record.

No way was I ready to go home. Instead, I went to the Cove, a beach close to my house. Bored? Go to the Cove. On a date? Go to the Cove. Want to soak in the sun while standing in the water? Go to the Cove. Need to make s'mores on a campfire? Go to the Cove. If you just found out you're pregnant and need to escape life to think? Go to the Cove.

I sat in the car, staring out over the water, pondering all that just happened. Praying, thinking, watching, worrying, then back to praying. Heck, someone could have written a song, calling it "Parked at the Cove." Verse after verse about dwelling on the new life ahead with all the worries built in. The chorus would repeatedly say something like, "The place to escape, pondering all your worries, out at the Cove."

While gazing at the water, I noticed a guy I graduated with walking up to my car door. *Oh, great. Of all the times for this kind of thing to happen! Not now,* I thought, while rolling my eyes as I rolled down the window.

"Hi, Bob. How ya doing?" I asked with a phony, like-I-cared, look. He started talking about college, work, and, of course, his love life. Thankfully he got interrupted by someone picking him up just as he asked me what I was up to. Man, what a relief!

I drove home, savoring the last few minutes of only me, realizing it was time to face perhaps the hardest thing, telling people I'm pregnant. I turned onto the dead-end street. The next-hardest thing was turning up my driveway.

CHAPTER 3
"Um, Mom, Dad"

As I walked in the front door, I couldn't help but wonder when to tell my parents that I was pregnant. Looking past the stairs and down the hall into the kitchen, I could see my dad sitting at the kitchen table reading the newspaper, while hearing my mom also in the kitchen, probably pouring more coffee for herself.

I, Marianne Extremely-Nervous Houstoun, headed down the hall. *No excuse why not to just tell them now.* However, my body turned to the left and headed up the stairs. *I still can't believe I have to tell my parents I'm pregnant. I'd better do it now and be done with it. I just hope they don't say something sarcastic about me and my, quote, Christian life.* Then, halfway up, I turned around and headed back down.

Okay, okay, here I go. Okay, I can do it. I can do it.

I can almost picture what I was wearing. Jeans, a long-sleeve shirt, and tennis shoes. The reason I remember my shoes is because, as I walked in, I was staring down at them while nervously holding my hands together. As my dad continued reading and my mom continued doing whatever she was doing in the kitchen, I began.

"Mom, Dad, I have something to, um, tell you." Dad looked up at me while still holding the paper as Mom stopped what she was doing and turned. I couldn't help but look back down at my shoes.

"Um, I'm... Something happened while in California. I'm... I'm pregnant."

I sort of expected one of them to at least say *something*. But instead, my mom, about six feet away, without saying a word, walked right over to me, arms out, and gave me a long hug. It was just what I needed. Wow. Nothing could have been better. More than anything in this entire book, that one hug has stayed glued to my heart the most all these years. Whenever I tell my story, one of the first things I say is how they both, to this day, have not made one negative comment about me messing up. Not one. Now don't think they instantly assumed everything would go peachy-keen for me, asking right off something like, "So, you want a boy or a girl?" No. They just learned from experience that love comes first; not teaching, not scolding, and no 'I told you so.'

They had learned from experience, as all their other daughters had this happen to them as well. I knew, however, that they considered this a totally different situation and loved me no matter what. True parental love.

We all stayed calm for the rest of the day. No deep talks about what I should do. But, don't think we were discussing what name to give it either. I shared with them what went on in California with Greg. You know, those things I didn't go out of my way to tell them the day I got back to town. They knew, however, that all I needed that night was warm, we're-here-for-you-no-matter-what, words. And that's good, because that's all I could really handle.

My mom, that evening, couldn't help but ask, "Are you up to eating what I'm making for dinner, or do you feel like eating something else?" I was soon to learn what she meant and why she asked that. Saying goodnight that night was followed by a warmer hug than normal.

As I got in bed, thinking so much about all that had gone on that day, my pillow began getting a bit damp with tears. Starting that day questioning if I was pregnant, to then going for a pregnancy test, to how should I tell my parents, to what should I do with this baby, my emotions were fried. In the dark, all by myself, it was difficult to soak in the fact that my life had changed and that I needed to face the fact that I have some very important decisions to make.

How can anyone go through this without God? God, I need you. Thankfully, I still felt peace, knowing God would do more than just stay right next to me on the long journey ahead. He would carry me.

The next morning, as usual, I went down into the living room. My mom, with her cigarette and coffee, was sitting in front of that fireless fireplace. As I walked in and sat on the couch, I couldn't help but wonder who would say what first as I noticed a few more-than-normal cigarette butts in the ashtray. As she was looking into the fireplace, I could tell she was pondering something. Of course, I knew what that something was.

"How did you sleep?" she asked, while seeming to look at me with a little more concern than usual.

Just great. Can't you see I'm having the time of my life? "Fine," I answered, having gotten all cozy on the couch and wishing I could stay there forever. Thankfully, I felt relaxed enough and okay to talk about this new issue we had to face. She asked the million-dollar question.

"So, Marianne, what are your thoughts on what you should do?"

I felt I knew what I should be doing and how I should do it as much as I knew how to write down in five seconds the answer to 7,459 divided by 3.7, in Roman numerals, eyes shut, with my hands behind my back.

"Oh, Mom, I don't know. I really don't."

Knowing my answer to that same question the day before had been to get an abortion and how that was now an impossibility for me, I was left with two options: keep the baby or give it up for adoption. It was weird, though. I remember sitting there, staring at the empty fireplace, not feeling as scared as I thought I should. Hard to explain. I don't mean to imply I had a couldn't-care-less attitude, but maybe now that the pregnancy-test worry was gone and the anxiety of telling my parents was over, the question of what I should do wasn't as difficult to think about. Perhaps having been around my sister, who's only three years older than me, and spending quite a bit of time with her two very young sons, caused me to feel that being around little kids was not so foreign. I don't know. I just had a willingness to at least *think* about keeping this baby.

Now who to tell?

I needed to tell the rest of my family. Thankfully, that went very well. I think since Kelly went through it all fairly recently, it wasn't really a new experience for them. All very supportive. A dear family. But what about my dearest of friends, Willma? Friends can be so different from family. Growing up with her down the street and sharing all of our woes and joys with one another for about twelve years by that point, she was obviously the first one outside of my family to tell.

But first, let's go back a few years. Many years, actually, to the day I met two important people in my life: Willma and Eyde Breakey. Most people make their best friends in school. Not me. One day, when I was eight years old and playing in my front yard, two girls who looked a few years older than me were just dillydallying around right by our driveway on the end of that dead-end street. I saw them; they saw me. *Ick! They have weird shorts on. Looks like they just cut their jeans above their knees. I'd never wear those!*

Eventually, we started talking.

"Hi, we just moved in," one said. More questions and facts began going back and forth.

"Where did you move from?"

"What's your name?"

"My name is Marianne. But my dad calls me Winnipoops."

"We found out we have a creek in our backyard. Do you?"

"I'm seven years old, the youngest of seven. Three brothers and three sisters."

"We have one older brother. We're both ten, because we're twins."

What? What did they say? Twins? But they don't look alike. I learned right then what fraternal twins are: twins who look nothing alike. That day began many years of a true friendship and the best example anyone could ask for of friends down the street.

Years later, God used those two to spark something new inside me: a new life. You see, the summer before I started college, the summer of '85, one year before that Fourth of July, was the summer that brought an end to one life and the beginning to another. My diary will give you hints of that change by revealing what I was like one month before I graduated, one month before that unforgettable, life-changing summer.

May 14, 1985

I'm on my journey to understanding Christianity and what Jesus can do for me. Eyde was first, but now Willma is very religious too! What is going on? Love with a man is nowhere to be found. I'm too young to find anyone again. Well, maybe not too young, but I depend on it too much. God will reward me, but WHEN? I believe in myself and feel I am a great person. (I sure was humble, wasn't I?) *I will write again when my questions are answered.*

As my diary shows, I felt empty at the end of my senior year, and my two dearest friends down the street, Eyde and Willma, were part of the reason why. They had both experienced something I had no real knowledge about: God's saving grace. But having seen this newness about them started questions flowing all through my brain, and for months my pillow continued to soak up all those thoughts. Then something happened the summer after I graduated. Feeling lonely and a bit sad about the uncertainty of this life ahead, I decided to accept Willma's invitation to attend a Christian camp.

I'm curious what this will be like. I'm Catholic, so I know God already. Heck, I even helped serve communion years ago. I'm good.

I know to obey God. I haven't done 'IT' with my past boyfriends, I don't really swear, and I work hard. I might be irked at God for having me weigh a bit more than I should, but, why is Willma so into this Christian stuff anyway? Oh, well. Maybe I'll understand more at this camp. After all, it's been a boring summer, and life here at home isn't so sweet. I wish Mom and Dad got along better.

That was another reason why I wanted to go to camp: I felt a need to escape life at home for a spell. Living at home with my parents in Normandy Park wasn't always peachy-keen, because my parents' relationship hadn't been going very well throughout my high school years. By then I learned the difference between getting along and, sad to say, not getting along. Thankfully, no ridiculous hatred or worry of harm was involved between my parents, but still, I knew their relationship was one of the reasons my mom often sat on the floor in front of the fireplace, with or without the fire going, cigarette in hand, ashtray by her side. That was where she started each day and ended each day, a place where she could let her thoughts go.

Me? My thoughts escaped on my pillow, up on my bed, night after night. Along with my dreams of what type of career I'd have, my pillow also knew the specifics of my dream about who and when I'd marry. Ready for that list? Marry the first man I fall in love with, have a six-month engagement leading to the most beautiful summertime wedding, him not seeing me wear my picture-perfect, dream-like wedding dress until I walked down the aisle, and make love for the first time on our wedding night, followed by living happily ever after.

It was at that camp, however, that God opened my eyes to a great realization. What He had given my friends months before, He also chose to give to me at that camp: love, forgiveness, peace, and best of all, a new heart. That weekend I learned what the word 'true' truly meant in regard to true repentance and what true forgiveness felt like. I knew God was now my true Father, the Holy Spirit was now planted inside me, and Jesus was right next to me for the rest of my life. I knew deep down that, as Psalm 40:2 describes, *God lifted me out of the slimy pit, out of the mud and mire; he set my feet on a rock and gave me a firm place to stand.*

As the group that had arrived there together began to drive away that last day, I looked back at the campground. *It's time I say goodbye to you, old self. I'm now my new me, very thankful to be on this new road ahead with Christ right by my side.* I came home not Marianne TV-Someone-Someday Houstoun, but as a peace-filled Marianne New-Child-of-God Houstoun.

Coming back home to a Catholic household wasn't easy, but God let me know He would help and guide me in that interesting, uncomfortable road ahead. Hunger for Christ had begun. As a few weeks went by, I learned that the saying 'God closes one door and opens another' is true, literally. The door to the Catholic church I grew up in closed as the door to a new church, a small, very warm, friendly, reformed Baptist church opened. I began attending, thanks to a friend of Willma's, Ralph. He had also just started going there. I began learning, and finally understanding, God's word. Willma and Eyde were out of town going to college at this point, so getting to know my new church family was priceless. As months went by, I learned so much from the messages and from mature Christians. I loved my new life, my new me.

Now you know why Willma was the next one to tell.

"Sure you can come over," Willma said after I called to see if we could get together. "It's pretty much lunchtime, so I'll start throwing a few sandwiches together."

I pondered how to tell her as I walked down to her house, that last house on our dead-end street. I knew it was just her there, so when I came up to the door, I took a deep breath.

Okay, here I go. While knocking lightly, I slowly opened the front door.

"Hi, Willma. I'm here. Where are —"

"Come on in. I'm back in the kitchen, right in the middle of making our lunch," she said as I walked in. Willma was her normal, cheery self. I could tell she was ready to talk away. Out of all the things in the world to talk about, she started talking about, gulp, the future. Half-joking but half-serious, she said, "Hey, Marianne, it's time we think more about when you and I move out. Let's figure out what college you or I'll be going to. What if you go to the same one I already go to?"

Breathe.

"We can try to get the same dormitory. Heck, the same room! Or maybe I'll work while you go there and we'll split the rent. I know, how about—"

As she was talking, so full of energy, my mind began filling to the brim with thoughts. You know how you can think of twenty different things in three seconds? Well, that's what I was doing. Sad to think how she and I wouldn't really be able to make many spur-of-the-moment plans as we had been doing for years. I was angry at myself for letting this happen, and a bit scared as to what this could do to our friendship. So much was being tossed around in my mind.

"Willma." It was obvious this was the time to tell her. "I have something I need to tell you. We can't really do that stuff you're talking about. because... I'm... I'm pregnant."

There, I did it. Now what? What will she say? What will she do?

She stopped what she was doing, frozen for two seconds, realizing I wasn't kidding.

"Oh. Uh, I guess we'll, um, have to alter our plans just a bit," she said calmly, a numb look on her face as she walked by with sandwich makings in her hands. Her look, however, instantly started changing, showing her mind forming different thoughts. I knew she would be shocked, and sure, I figured her emotions would be zig-zagging in all different directions. Thankfully, though, as

I shared the entire story with her, I could tell her thoughts were getting straight once again.

While eating that lunch, I heard my best friend tell me she'd be there for me and how God would not let go of me. Not really hearing those types of words from my family, hearing it from her was priceless. The more we discussed the pros and cons of keeping or adoption, we both leaned toward me keeping the baby. No decisions whatsoever on what to do regarding money, the baby's father, work, and other matters. Just on whether I should be the mother of this baby.

As I was walking out that same door I came in, I felt God had used my friend as a means for guidance and a means to give me strength. My name was changed once again on my walk home. Marianne A-Bit-More-Peace-To-Keep-Baby Houstoun

Okay, now who? Who should I tell next? I still can't believe I'm pregnant.

Three days since that pregnancy test. Three long days. I was sort of glad there were another three days until church, but then I also wished it were only one. I needed to get together with my fellow church family. Since it had been a little over a week that I'd been home from California and had only gone to church once since being back, I wasn't ready to just walk on in and shout, "Hi, everyone! I'm pregnant!" Telling the pastor first was my plan, but I still had to wait until Sunday.

What I was putting on the back burner those days was telling Greg. Ugh. Did I need to include the one who *got* me pregnant? Why can't I just not tell him? After all, when I left I didn't even say, "We'll keep in touch" or "Talk to ya later." Nope. Our relationship was done, or so I thought.

Now seems as good a time as any to tell how this relationship began. About eight months after that camp, four months before that Fourth of July, my second quarter at the community college was close to ending in the spring of 1986. My goal in life was to one day work either behind or in front of the TV screen. Being an actress or director, someday, was my dream. But those two quarters of college had nothing to do with that dream.

I don't feel I really need these classes. Reading comprehension? Math 101? Why not TV 101 or Be-Seen-On-The-Screen 101? What to do, what to do? I don't wanna waste time with useless classes.

Okay, not totally useless, but as I had just turned nineteen, I felt I needed to escape it all for a while and ponder more on what I wanted to do with my life. As months went by, church was still great and I was getting closer to the people there. But besides that, nothing kept me from taking the offer Debbie, an older friend of mine in California, made.

"Oh, Debbie, I really don't feel like wasting time with such useless classes. Plus, home here with Mom and Dad sure isn't full of fun," I vented, knowing my parents were contemplating the thought of separating. Plus, here in town, my sister Janis's five-year-old daughter, Brenda, was very ill, and it was questionable how long she had to live. Perhaps only a few months.

"Well, you could come stay with me for a while and see what happens," Debbie said. "I'd love to help. It would be cool, us sharing my apartment."

The phone cord kept me from bouncing on my bed. "Hey, I love that idea! Why not?" We discussed how to make it work and how, after finding a job, I'd then help pay the rent. Perfect plan! I knew I'd need to find a church, realizing I needed God in California just as much as I needed Him in Washington.

I felt mature enough (as I bet most nineteen-year-olds do) to leave home, and I got all excited thinking about the possibilities. The timing was perfect, since I was finishing my second quarter and the beautiful spring-like feel was at hand. My parents were not so gung-ho, but being I was nineteen, they couldn't stop me, and, thankfully, they trusted me. They felt I wouldn't be stupid enough to do something foolish. My brother Bud, living close to where I'd be, helped my parents feel more comfortable with the plan.

Finally... *I can't believe it. My last night at home. I'm sure it'll all go fine. It has to go fine. It'll be interesting living with Debbie, but she's so sweet. I bet she'll help me find a job since she knows what's around there. Weird leaving Seattle, but I can't wait to see what it's like living in California. Hope I find some cool place to work. Maybe cuter guys are there, too. Wonder how nervous I might get being on my own to find a church. Glad I'm all packed so I can start driving first thing in the morning. Pretty sure I have that big map in the car already. God, please help me know what I'm doing.*

I was ready to take off in my own little car the next morning.

God, gas, and a bag of chips: check. Map, clothes, toothbrush, Bible, oh, and of course my pillow: check. Goodbye, house, goodbye, Mom and Dad. Goodbye, you little town of Normandy Park. Hello, new world!

After that first day's long drive, all the goodies were gone and I had gotten tired of listening to the twenty-million tapes I brought. Even having CDs back then would have been better. If I could have just connected an iPhone. But, oh well. Fast forward was the only way to skip the boring songs. One thing's for sure, knowing God was by my side as I camped out at a cheap motel that one night sure helped.

I can remember that next day, those maps I brought spread out all over the passenger seat. Having a Google map on a cell phone sure would have been useful then. A few pay phones were necessary to reach Debbie, as well. Finally, I drove up to her—I mean my—I mean our—place. Debbie was a good, protective friend, about ten years older, who helped me adjust to my new surroundings. I loved discussing how we'd work out all the food bills, whose stuff was whose, and who did what.

Now please keep in mind, I was far from being considered a mature Christian and, sad to say, wasn't secure enough yet to really open up with others about God and what He had graciously done for me. I knew she didn't go to any church, so I just played it safe and didn't bring up anything that sounded religious.

A few days later, while driving around my new town, I saw a sign. *What? That brand-spanking-new hotel is hiring? AWESOME!* Inside I went. Right then and there I filled out the paperwork. As the lady read it, she said it looked pretty promising that I could be a waitress, but she had to follow the rules and wait for an interview. I started working there a few days later.

"Mom, guess what?" I burst out as soon as she answered the phone, "I GOT A JOB!" and on I went, telling her every little detail. She was so excited for me.

I felt proud of having the important responsibility of being a waitress at a nice restaurant in this elegant hotel. All of us new waiters and waitresses, all close in age, hit it off from the start.

"I can do this!" I thought. It seemed so sudden, but I sure didn't mind. I enjoyed meeting all these new people, working in an impressive hotel, living in a cool little apartment, and feeling like I was starting a new life. Not a TV job, but at least I wasn't wasting my time taking useless classes. I loved this newness in my life. I didn't, however, pay attention to a red light that was flashing inside my heart.

Nothing Christ-centered was around me. Sure, I felt like I should find some sort of church, but before I knew it, weeks went by. No one at work was standing up on the table saying "I'm saved!" and I wasn't very bold in sharing that I was, either. Everyone was nice to me, and that's all I thought I needed. But I did have the constant nagging thought that I should find a church. No Googling Baptist-church-California back then. Just a simple look in the yellow pages. I even tried out one Baptist church, but only once. Basically, I got a bit too lazy. *I'll just make sure I read my Bible. That's good enough for now.*

At work I found myself being just a wee bit happier around this one guy, Greg, who was twenty years old and living with his parents. We talked a lot and got along great. Before too long we found ourselves going out to grab lunch during our break. Then again the next day and the next. And after a few times doing that, it was getting dinner after work. It was becoming obvious we were an item, sort of. We never really talked about dating, but we both, and others, sensed this was going somewhere. After a few more days went by, he offered to take me around town, show me cool places I hadn't seen yet. I loved the thought.

"Do you mind picking me up?" he asked. "No car of my own yet."

"Sure, no problem. Just jot down your address."

Cruising around was great, enjoying the many beautiful places around town. As the hours went by, I found myself falling head over heels in like with him. But I started to have a worry. I knew I should only be considering a Christian man to have a relationship with.

When we were done driving around, I felt it was time to be bold and say something. Sort of sad, because I liked him, but I knew I had to see if he and I were like-minded about God. I sort of assumed he wasn't, but I hadn't shared anything about what I believed yet either. Man, this was all new to me.

We pulled up to his house and parked. *I have to talk with him. Better now than never.*

"Greg. I, um... have to say something," I said as I looked straight out the front window of my car, staring at the front window of his house. "There's something about me that I have to tell you. You see, I'm a Christian, and even though it looks like you and I are becoming more than just friends, we can't if you're not a Christian." There, I said it. "And if you have not committed your heart to God..."

"Oh, no need to worry. I've been a Christian for a while now," was his response.

"Really?" Oh, what a sigh of relief. "How did it happen?" I was so eager to hear his story.

"Less than a year ago we had some relatives in town, and they go to church. They wanted to go while in town, so I went with them, but only because my parents made me. The pastor ended the sermon by saying that if anyone wanted to be saved, you just needed to raise your hand, walk down here, and pray with everyone. I didn't really care about that part, but this cute girl I knew from school that I've always liked was on the same pew I was on. So when I saw she raised her hand, I wanted her to notice me, so I raised my hand. What was nice was she and I walked down to the altar next to each other. Nothing between us came from that, as I had hoped. But since I raised my hand, walked with the others, and said whatever it was I had to, that saved me."

Man, was I stupid back then. I just wanted to believe anything that would make him a Christian. I believed that what he had done was perhaps all that was needed. After all, how God saved me wasn't totally normal, so heck, God could have saved Greg that way.

"Oh, good! That's great!" I said with the biggest sigh of relief as we talked more about it. I then shared my testimony with him. We were a bit shy all of a sudden, but soon started grinning and then laughing, knowing we were now in total agreement that we wanted to spend even more time with each other. Perfect time, right then and there, for us to give that first quick smooch to officially show we were a couple. Many days of bliss followed, and that bliss is what helped me not hold too much against him for asking THE question: "Why are your hands so wrinkly?"

Perhaps I should explain what in the world made him say that. My mother's side of the family passed along to me wrinkly hands. (Darn it, the only one of us seven Houstoun siblings to inherit that trait.) So, sure enough, that question, "Why are your hands so wrinkly?" was one I got used to, and tired of, having heard it for years. And one more thing that was a bit tough to deal with, especially in high school: I was about fifteen pounds or so overweight. Thankfully, though, I was a bit taller than most others, five foot eight, so it wasn't too embarrassing to be a bit heavy. I admit, working at Winchell's Donuts during high school didn't help.

Since I'm sharing a few more things about me here, I'll throw one more in. You already know about me not having a middle name, but you don't yet know I've never liked coffee. Nope. Sorry. No thanks. I'm proud to say that, even though all my siblings followed in my parents' footstep, at least liking, if not loving, coffee, I never had an interest in it. 'No thanks' was my simple answer whenever asked.

Back at work people could tell Greg and I were now an item. I was, however, sensing that little red light flashing in my soul as a few weeks went by, but I managed to ignore it. I wanted to believe I knew what I was doing, having him as my boyfriend. After all, remember, I was mature.

The first warning sign was one beautiful sunny afternoon. My first time going into his house. "No reason not to meet my parents now," he said. "I'm sure they want to finally meet who they keep hearing about."

"Great, I'd love to meet them," said Marianne Nervous-As-Can-Be Houstoun.

"They should be home soon. Here, let me show you our backyard," said Greg.

Nice yard, indeed. A perfect place to chat while sitting on a bench. A perfect place to pull my Bible out, thinking since he and I had a bit of time to kill, why not show him a few of my favorite verses? I was so excited to have a Christian relationship going, thinking we should do things like that. He should appreciate me wanting to share a chapter that meant so much to me.

"Hey, Greg, there's something I've been reading and want to share with you. Here, let me read you this verse," I said while pulling my Bible out of my tote bag. He sat still for a few verses, but I could tell he had absolutely no interest. I felt a little sadness forming inside me. Before I knew it, he grabbed my Bible, dropped it, and started kissing me. I just laughed and started kissing him back, knowing I was wasting my time reading. While that was going on, I tried to deny the emptiness I was feeling inside.

Shouldn't he have shown at least some sign of interest? Greg says he's a Christian. I'd want a man to show at least a little interest in the Bible. Oh, well.

Thankfully, we heard his parents drive up soon after that, and I was glad because it got me thinking about something else. Meeting his parents for the first time began to fill that emptiness. A very warm greeting started an enjoyable conversation in that nice, clean, family atmosphere.

As a few more weeks went by, I got to visit with his parents another time or two. I liked them. We talked about my family, Greg's family, and what it had been like for me in Seattle. I didn't bring up any religious topics, however, as Greg had told me the day we exchanged our testimonies that he had never told his parents what had happened that one day at church. I promised I would not say a word.

A few days later, Greg turned twenty-one.

"Marianne, how about we celebrate? Let me buy us some beer."

"Hey, why not?" I love this adult-like feeling. This will be just fine. Since most people are surprised when I tell them I'm only nineteen, I might as well act older. I'm not one who would get drunk, so hey, what's one beer? Heck, maybe even two.

He loved buying that six pack before we headed to my apartment to watch TV, knowing Debbie would be gone for a few hours. (People would go crazy now if they had only six or seven channels like we did back then.) Problem. The TV was in my bedroom. What started as sitting up next to each other with our backs against the wall, each with a beer in hand, watching whatever was on, slowly led to relaxing a bit too much on that bed.

I'm sure you've heard the saying, 'One thing leads to another.' Sad to say, that fits perfectly here. Starting with just watching TV, sitting all nice and cozy, caused one little kiss to take place, which then turned into something that went way too far and way too fast. It's a shame to admit that I let my heart overrule what my mind was telling me. Guilt started bubbling up. Drowning with the shame of admitting that I was, right then and there, doing what I thought only incredibly weak or sex-crazed women did. Worse yet, I knew I was not following God's expectations. All these thoughts I was having were overruled by my hormones. *This is fine. No, it's not. Yes, it is. No, it's not.* Those thoughts ping-ponged back and forth in my mind as things were getting way overheated. *How? How did this get so far?* My mind raced as I searched for answers that didn't exist as to how and why most of my attire had made it to the floor.

Let's see, how can I word this and leave it rated PG? How about by saying my goal of waiting for my wedding night was ruined. I instantly felt shame and guilt. Yes, it happened. I lost my virginity.

When all was said and done, with that phony clean-conscience-looking smile, it was time for him to leave. Being dark outside and still dark inside, I made sure the only light was from the TV—easier for me to hide my guilt. We gave each other a little kiss as he walked out the door, me covered with a blanket. Finally, I was by myself. I refused to cry.

It's not that bad. I'll be fine. I'll just tell him absolutely no more. Easy.

As my head hit the pillow that night, I felt ashamed. Having sex with Greg was nowhere to be found on my list of things to do when that day started. So what happened? I didn't love him, so then why did it happen? How did it happen? For the first time ever, the enormous guilt of sin pounded in my heart. I'm sure my pillow sensed those heavy, guilt-ridden thoughts my mind was carrying. Tears began. *God, please. Please forgive me.*

That next day I felt like, excuse my language, crap, with a capital C. I had no confidence in myself to be what I hoped I'd be: a strong follower of Christ. A good Christian? Yeah, right. A mature adult? Who knows when I'd ever come close to being one. No claiming ignorance about God's thoughts on all this. I saw my sin and pleaded for His forgiveness. But still, when would I stop feeling like the dirtiest dirt-ball in the universe?

I dreaded the next time I'd see Greg. It's not like I wanted to go out of my way and call him. I'm sure if there were cell phones back then, I would have had mine turned off. I remember thinking of reasons not to be at my apartment, because if I wasn't, then I couldn't hear the phone ring, right?

Those fifty or so stores I haven't been to yet do sound really interesting today.

I was so relieved the next day when I went to work and he wasn't there. I even avoided calling him the following day. But, of course, it finally happened. It was just a few days later he stopped by to take me out for a bite to eat. Nothing was said about what took place those few nights back except some humorous comment here or there. A simple kiss goodbye, one I easily could have done without.

As a few more days went by, new thoughts were forming. I was nineteen and still had a very big desire to have a career with photos and/or making movies. But in order to do that, I couldn't just stay here and work in a restaurant. I knew, at the drop of a hat, my parents would help me get back into school. And I really did miss church. That one church I visited in California was far from anything I wanted. Also, I changed my mind, after all, that maybe I should be close to Brenda, who was still very close to dying. Funny how our reasoning can change because of guilt. And I even missed the cooler, damp weather back home.

Okay, I confess. I just didn't want to be around that guilt-filled atmosphere anymore. I had to leave. Sure, Greg was still nice and all, but that one night showed me he wasn't the man God wanted for me. God, school, God, school, the only two things I should really focus on. Oh, maybe one more thing. Canceling the California license plate I had ordered a week prior.

Deciding to move back turned into me kissing my relationship with Greg goodbye, literally. He seemed a bit confused as to why I wanted to go back home. I just said the pros for leaving far outweighed the cons.

Smooch.

Goodbye.

Good riddance.

Thankfully, saying goodbye to Debbie went fine. I think she sort of missed living on her own, but more so understood that it was better for me to move back. And no, she didn't know about the main reason for my leaving.

I had the best adventure driving back home, because this time my brother Bud, who lived not too far from where I stayed with Debbie, tagged along. God knew I needed him with me, because what I thought would be a two-day drive from California back to Seattle turned into five.

I will never forget that Saturday morning, stopping by a simple restaurant for breakfast after staying the night before at a small hotel. Just as we began nibbling on our eggs, knowing we'd start our last day driving as soon as we were done, we looked out the window.

"Nice we got to park right in front of the window here," Bud said as we were handed our breakfast. We began eating. And I had orange juice while he had his coffee.

"Um, Bud, look at that front tire on my car. Does it look weird to you?" I asked after taking a few bites.

He looked. I looked. We both noticed that one front tire was quickly losing air. We instantly turned to each other and, without saying a word, began inhaling our eggs. As we shoved them down our throats, we began laughing.

We had to wait until the following Monday before we could get a new tire and finish our drive home. Neither one of us will ever forget that unexpected mini-vacation filled with a couple rented bikes, watching movies, munching on snacks, and silly talks about using our dad's VISA number for all this fun. I think God knew I needed to escape all that had happened the past few weeks, and He was giving me a breather before starting the rough road ahead—and I'm not talking about the freeway.

So there I was, about to call a twenty-one-year-old who had no real goals in life and who had no noticeable ambition for a career. A man I did not love but whose child I was carrying.

I don't want to, but I should. I should. I know I should, but… but…

Part of me just wanted to get it out of the way and over with. The other part? *I'll call for sure… tomorrow.* My parents were very supportive either way, keeping the baby or giving it up for adoption. They did let me know, though, that it was my responsibility to tell Greg, and they encouraged me not to wait.

Ring, ring. Ring, ri…

"Hello." It was him. It hit me hard. It's him.

"Hello." *Does he recognize my voice?* "Is this Greg?"

"Yes, it is. Is this Marianne?" I could tell from his tone of voice that he was surprised.

"Yes, it is."

"Oh. Well, hello."

Should I talk about the weather for a spell? No.

"If you're wondering why I'm calling, I'm calling to let you know I'm pregnant and that the baby is yours."

Silence.

"You're… pregnant?" A little space between those words.

"Yes."

Silence. I knew I needed to allow him a little time to breathe and come out of shock, but finally I had to say something. I said, a bit slower than normal, "So, what are you thinking?"

His answer showed that he didn't know what in the world *to* think. I was rather bold and told him right up front that an abortion was not an option. I could tell he was disappointed, but thankfully he didn't make a big deal about that decision. A sudden trap, I'm sure he felt.

We ended the talk by agreeing to go through this together, but that he would wait to hear from me on what I decided to do. I was a bit sad that there was no bold, mature, adult response like, "No matter what, I'm right by your side and will aim at making this the best thing for us both. I love you and will do anything that's best for our baby. I'm eager to meet your parents to show them I will take care of us all." Instead, he had a more of a "yeah, whatever" attitude. I just told myself that it was better he be that way than have some selfish, mean, I-don't-care attitude. He agreed it was his responsibility to do something, even if it meant we would get married and keep the baby.

Me? Get married? Now? I knew I didn't want to decide right then over the phone, so I told him I'd get back with him in a few days. I hung up, telling myself the talk went pretty well. But I also found myself needing to find something good out of everything lately.

After hanging up the phone, I felt like hiding from the world for a while. My thoughts of deciding what to do had begun, but they were too hard to share with anyone. I could give the baby up for adoption and have no further connection with Greg; have the baby and not get married; or have the baby and get married. I didn't want to hear from anyone right then, and I didn't feel like deciding. I just wanted God to tell me.

Mom and Dad know – check
My siblings know – check
Willma knows – check
Greg knows – check
Pastor Mark was next on the list. A few days of nothing to do

and no one to tell were much needed. My pillow must have noticed my head wasn't so heavy with the worry of telling anyone. It did, however, sense more of my thoughts on what was forming inside of me and if I should keep him or her.

Time now just to ponder and pray over what I should do. The more I talked with my mom, Willma, and my sister Kelly, the more support I was feeling in keeping the baby.

God, tell me what to do, please.

I knew I couldn't really decide this totally on my own. I needed some pastoral advice. Sunday morning had arrived. Having been gone two months didn't weaken the friendships I had made at church before I left. But still, I wasn't comfortable enough to just march on in, stand in front of everybody and say, "Hi, guys. A funny thing happened to me in California."

After walking in and saying hi to friends, I sat down. The only thing I could think about was when would be the right time to talk to Pastor Mark. He and his wife were expecting their first baby at that time, so I thought at least he could sort of understand a bit of what I was dealing with. During the entire service I could only think about what his first words would be after I told him. How would he reply? Will I be to him some foolish Christian with the words *"Still a Sinner"* spray-painted on her forehead? From then on would he just feel sorry for me whenever he'd see me? Would he stare straight at me whenever he would bring up the words "sex before marriage" in a sermon? I sure wasn't having encouraging thoughts.

By the time the service was done and the last hymn was being sung, I had my plans down pat. Allow him to talk with a few people and wait for him to head back to his office to get his things before he heads out.

I enjoyed talking about my outing to California with a few I hadn't told the week before. However, telling people was different this week than last, being that I had a totally different fact stored inside. The fact that I was carrying a baby was just a hair different from last week's "hmm, I really hope I start my period today." As I talked, I kept an eye on Pastor Mark to keep track of where he was.

There he goes to get his things from the office. Okay, Marianne, now. I excused myself from the small group I was talking with.

"Hi, Pastor Mark. Do you have a few minutes? I need to talk to you."

"Sure. Now would be fine. We can just stay here if you want." We both knew the few others still there were far enough away so as not to overhear. I'll be honest, I remember exactly where we stood, but I don't remember word for word what I said, and I know why. It's because the way he responded fully outweighed that uneasiness of however I said it.

"Marianne, the first thing I want you to know is that if you have truly asked God for forgiveness… Have you?"

I made sure he knew how much sorrow I felt and how I had pleaded with God to forgive me.

"Well, then God has forgiven you, Marianne. Please don't let the weight of sin make it tougher for you. God loves you, and as long as you have asked, truly asked for forgiveness, He has forgiven you and will carry you through it."

Part of me just wanted him to tell me if I should marry the father or not, even while knowing that he couldn't. I'm sure if he had known Greg, he would have felt more able to guide me, but he didn't, so he couldn't. He basically reminded me to have an ear for what others have to say, but don't be forced by anyone.

"Marianne, follow what you feel you should do and pray for God's guidance, but make sure you don't let your emotions overrule you. Just remember God will care for you. Like Philippians 4:6 says, 'Be anxious for nothing, but in everything by prayer and supplication, with thanksgiving, let your requests be made known to God.'"

Easier said than done, of course, but what he said and how he said it was immensely helpful and encouraging.

Now came the time we needed to end our conversation, as most people had left, but he insisted on ending with prayer. His kind look and tone of voice came to me as a shepherd caring for his sheep. Once again, God showing me, this time via Pastor Johnson, He was carrying me and not just holding my hand.

That night my pillow sensed the extra peace I was feeling as I lay down and prayed, thanking God for showing me, through that talk, that He forgave me. Oh, what peace that brought.

CHAPTER 4
Decision Made

Okay, the world knew I was pregnant. Now what? *Everyone could now call me Marianne Preg-O Houstoun for a little more than seven months.*

A few things had me leaning toward keeping the baby instead of giving it up for adoption. Seeing Kelly, often with her two little boys, convinced me how doable it was. And my parents offering to support me, saying I could live there as long as needed, was another main reason. Having the pastor and his wife also due with their first baby very soon helped me decide, knowing I wouldn't be going through it alone. Those verses Pastor Mark shared with me sure were encouraging. Night after night, morning after morning, I pondered that important decision over and over again on my pillow. Me, a mom. I got used to that thought.

Take a deeeeeeep breath. The decision had been made. *I think I can do it. I will keep this baby.* The most-important decision I've ever made. Thankfully, I felt much peace with my choice.

Time now for that second in line of most-important decisions: Should I marry Greg or raise this child on my own? *If I do marry him, then when? Now, or after the baby's born? Here, or in California? If here, how involved would his parents be?* (Breeeeeeathe.) *Would I stay at home while he works or would we both work? If we don't marry, then how long until I find a job? I know I could get financial help. Will I be able to spoil myself once in a blue moon or would any extra money go toward a babysitter?*

The next question sort of umbrellaed over all the others: What does God want me to do? Night after night before falling asleep, or morning after morning before getting up, my pillow could sense I was praying, asking God to guide me in this decision. I'd be surprised if my pillow didn't start praying as well, as it sensed such an important question.

This is where history interrupted. Growing up, I had it molded inside me to think that it's the pregnant woman's responsibility to marry the father. No ifs, ands, or buts. After all, if the two caused the problem and if the two can at least tolerate one another, then the two must bite the bullet and get married. The baby needs both its parents.

Not really knowing anyone else who had gone through this aside from my sisters, I basically felt I should do what they did and get married. I decided that it would be best to marry Greg. And I added the thought that marrying Greg could be God's tool in saving him.

I liked thinking that perhaps, just perhaps, God did have me as His tool to save Greg. As I shared with my family the thought of keeping the baby, I got their support. A few "are you sure's" were asked, of course. Friends from church also supported my decision to marry. "Are you sure?" was common from many there as well, along with "Let me know how I can help with the wedding." Not one negative response.

But the main thing that kept me going, besides the support from family and friends, was knowing that God would guide me. What I needed most was the feeling that God would make it all work out, somehow, someway.

"Mom, when do you think we should get married?" I asked her as she stared at the empty fireplace, cigarette in hand. "Months from now? After the baby's born?"

"I'm thinking more like one or two months, before you get too worn out and looking too pregnant. But for sure not after you have it. The baby needs a normal family life as soon as he or she comes home."

I understood her thoughts and agreed. Time to call. (Darn it.)

"Yeah, I guess that sounds like what we should do," Greg said after I shared with him what I felt was best for us all. Kind of quiet again, just like it was when I originally told him I was pregnant. Now, I didn't really expect him to jump for joy about my thoughts on what we should do. Time for another dream-on response. "I want to marry you no matter what reason we have. You are the only one in this entire world I will ever want to marry." Instead, it was more like, "Okay, if you think we should. I'll go tell my parents right now and call ya back." It wasn't even an hour before he called back. He didn't sound much better about it all, but thankfully he didn't sound worse. His parents also agreed we should get married soon.

"So you'll fly here in a few weeks, and we'll aim to get married two or three weeks later. Sound good?" I asked.

"Sounds good," he said, without much of a joy-filled sound in those words.

Lying in bed that night, my pillow sensed I was praying. *God, please show me You're pleased with my decision. I guess now that it's been decided to marry him, You must have wanted us to. Oh, God, I hope I'm right.*

It felt like my pillow cried a few tears along with mine. After all, it had known my dream-wedding ideas for years as well, but also knew I was going to a thrift store the next day to look for a cheap wedding dress to wear at a very simple wedding after a four-week engagement to a man I knew I didn't love. My pillow and I had realized that dream wedding was now dumped in the trash and that I was nowhere near marrying the first man I loved, or wearing the type of dress I'd like to frame, plus nowhere near six months till the 'I dos' would be exchanged. And, worse yet, not waiting till the wedding night to make love for the first time, which caused all this mess in the first place. Nothing close to my dream wedding.

"Marianne, really, it looks great on you," Mom said as we

stepped out of this somewhat uninviting thrift store, the last of many we had checked out. I acted as if I liked the store, but only because I knew she did. And I knew all this was hard for her too. I'm sure she could tell what I was feeling inside as she witnessed me staring away at nothing in the store as I kept wondering if all this was right. *How. In. The. World can I wear this?* But then I would shake my head.

"Oh, it's fine, Mom. Really. After looking around at so many, this one is the best. White, sweet, and simple." *But still icky.*

Oh, you don't even want me to describe that wedding dress we found. Remember, I was already a bit overweight, so to find a wedding dress I'd even like, let alone love, that fit, in a small thrift store, was like finding a perfect ice cube in the middle of the desert. No miracle that day. A simple white dress was all we could find. Mom could sense how I was feeling, so she, on our way home, splurged and bought me some spankin'-new jewelry to go with it. To this day I remember the cute little jewelry box I kept those earrings and that necklace in.

One week now until Greg would fly up. One week left to pretend there was no huge change about to happen in my life. An entire week to enjoy me, myself, and I. No one I had to hang around with. No one I had to force myself to be comfortable around. Only me, my pillow, and this child I was carrying. God was so helpful even in that area. No morning sickness at all. Yep. I repeat, no morning sickness. Sure, an occasional slightly nauseous feeling, but nothing like I had been warned about. Well, maybe once. I'll never forget the one—I repeat—one time I did throw up. It was late in the afternoon after eating a can of fruit I was craving. Peaches, to be exact. Obviously I didn't crave them anymore after that—how shall I say it?—quaint time leaning over the sink, letting those peaches pop back out. Seeing canned peaches in stores now always brings back that memory.

My pillow could sense I was growing with uncertainty as that week went by. It could tell it was my favorite place to be that week. Willma was away at college and wasn't there for me to escape with, and I wasn't yet good enough friends with people from church to just hang out. I mostly stayed around the house, up in my bedroom, time and time again lying on my back, staring up at the celling.

I can't believe I'll be a mom soon and even sooner be married to a man I really don't want to marry. What will my family think of him? What will people at church think of him? More importantly, what does God think of him?

I tried to convince myself that all would go fine, and after time, he would find out the TRUE meaning of being saved and we would live happily ever after.

Oh, my word. Flight's on time, I thought as I called to check on his arrival. *Great. Time to act like I'm all excited to see him.* Was I happy at all? Just a wee bit, because, after all, I did like him a lot before, but, well, you know the rest. I was still a bit more sad than happy, though, because I knew I was about to start the rest of my life in a way I hadn't really hoped for or planned on.

SeaTac Airport, not even five minutes from my house. I remember wishing, while driving, that it would take forever to get there. As I drove, I was pleading with God for help on how I would react as soon as I'd see Greg. I wished I were just driving to the airport like I did my senior year in high school, flying to visit my oldest sister in Florida. Or, better yet, going back to when I worked as a driver for Doug Fox Travel, where I picked up customers from the airport to take them to their cars. I really wished that's all I was doing right then. But no, I was about to pick up the man I would soon marry.

Time to park, walk into the airport, and look for Greg. His flight had landed and people were now getting off. That day was way before nine-eleven, so you were able to watch the plane pull up and stop and then wait patiently to see people get off the plane. Passenger after passenger walked in, either being greeted by family or friends or looking for the sign pointing to where to get their luggage.

If you're like me, you can picture the parts of a movie when something happens and all of a sudden the movie goes into slow motion. That part of this story is now. In slow motion I see Greg make that turn at the boarding gate and step into the airport, slowly looking around for me. Seems like it took forever for him to see me, but then I didn't really go out of my way to be noticed. I knew that as soon as he saw me, that slow-motion scene would end and I'd be back to real life. Yes, I hoped I looked nice, and I was glad I didn't look pregnant yet. Thankfully, too, he wasn't someone really hard to be around, along with being on the handsome side. I just knew in my heart that I was a Christian, he wasn't, and that I needed God's help.

Our eyes met. *Come on, Marianne, grin. You're getting married in a few weeks.* I waved. The slow motion stopped. Right then I felt a door was shutting behind me as I walked forward into this new life ahead.

Of course we were both nervous. I knew it was hard for him, as well, in facing all this. We gave each other a hug that sort of tested us to see if we could believe this was really happening. My first real sentence to him was, "So how was your flight?" as if it really mattered or I was really concerned. Off we went to get his luggage, surrounded by other people as we watched all those suitcases dropping off and going around the carousel.

"There's mine," he said, stretching out to grab it. I couldn't help but think how that luggage he was grabbing would soon be part of my own life. I might as well consider that my suitcase too. Cute, but not the most heartwarming thought.

Having so many people around helped give us a good reason why we couldn't just jump into talking about our new life ahead. No complaining. It helped us both get a little more used to each other before it would be just the two of us in my car.

It sure helped me being the one driving *my* car, to *my* house, with *my* family, in *my* neighborhood. But Greg, he just left *his* home, *his* family, *his* friends, and *his* family car. I started feeling sorry for him as he shut the car door. *How uncomfortable he must be feeling right now, knowing he's about to meet everyone in my world.* I remember asking God, as I drove us to my house, to please help him not feel so uncomfortable with this big change.

Remember how I wished it would be a longer drive to go pick him up? Now I was glad it was a really short drive back to the house. It meant only a few uncomfortable minutes in the car. We talked about the weather for a while, but as the moments went by, we started talking a bit about who he'd meet that day. On second thought, maybe it wasn't so great for it to be short. Time now for him to meet my family. The look on his face showed great nervousness. "It'll be okay. Let's go in," I said.

Again, I was sure glad we were walking into *my* house. As I opened the door, I began wondering how Greg would act when he saw my dad, and vice versa. My dad was, as usual, sitting at the kitchen table reading the paper. As we walked into the kitchen, my dad looked up, put the newspaper down, and, with a kind, warm smile, stood up and started walking our way. *Oh, this is weird.*

All went fine, for the most part. Greg was a little too shy, I thought, but I was no pro at knowing what to expect. Sure, the "So how was your flight?" question was again asked. It's sort of like the first layer that needs to be taken off whenever you meet someone for the first time. As every minute goes by, a new layer is taken off in hopes of reaching a definite comfort level. Many layers to go.

When the flight talk was done, I wanted to avoid any awkwardness and asked, "So, where's Mom?"

"She'll be back soon. Had to hit a store." Knowing my mom, she probably knew little finger snacks would be good to have so a few nervous hands would have something to do.

We went outside. I could tell Greg was a bit more relaxed as we walked around the backyard. "Your dad seems pretty nice," he said, which then led to a bit more serious talk as we headed down to the creek about how hard it was for him to leave his place in

California. It wasn't like we were all ready to just chit-chat away about everything, but it was getting better.

We decided to go back inside so I could show him where to put his stuff. But once inside, we heard *the* sound. *The* automatic garage door starting to open.

"My mom's here," I said as I quickly guided him to the TV room where she would come in from the garage. Nervousness ignited. The garage door stopped. It was all the way up and you could now hear the car pulling in. I grabbed his hand to get him to stand next to me so as to be ready when my mom came in.

"I am so nervous," he said, all weak-kneed.

Oh, REALLY? As if I couldn't tell as he slid behind me.

"Oh, Greg, stop that!" He was still behind me. "Greg, come on!" I said, as if I were a commander-in-chief. "Be REAL and stand NEXT to me!"

Having seen my car in the driveway, I was sure my mom knew Greg and I were there as the garage door closed. As we both stared at the door, seeing the inside doorknob turning, Greg quickly moved behind me once again.

Stop. Hold everything. When meeting her mother, shouldn't a twenty-one-year-old man stand bravely next to the woman he is soon to marry? Why is this man acting like a young boy who thinks he's about to see a spooky monster?

As I was grinding my teeth, trying to move my body back while still trying to force him to move forward next to me, the door opened. I couldn't believe this was happening. It took me only a fraction of a second to wish he would just disintegrate. *And to think I'm about to MARRY this kid!* My last attempt at pulling him to stand next to me was a success as the door was then totally opened, with my mom standing right there, a grocery bag on one arm and her purse on the other. As she walked in, because of the look on her face I could sense she was wondering why our faces were a bit stressed. She put the bag down as I tried to calmly say, "Hi, Mom."

Looking directly at him, she responded with, "You must be Greg. Glad to meet you."

I had to give him a little nudge on the side to get him to even say something. I was overcome with embarrassment, even though he did manage to say, "Hello, Mrs. Houstoun. Glad to meet you too."

Mature? No. Childish? Yes. All I could do was roll my eyes and have a few thoughts go through my head that I really shouldn't write.

My mom was so nice, however, in how she responded. Yes, she too made that safe hope-your-flight-was-okay comment while she grabbed the grocery bag to go down the hall. As we walked behind my mom on the way to the kitchen, I remember looking into the laundry room, wishing I were ten years younger when the only hard thing to do then was fight with my brother David in that room. The fighting was about whose turn it was to take care of Sam, our dog, and fill his food and water bowl that used to be on the floor in there. But no, we three, plus my dad, were now in the kitchen.

Mom grabbed a bag of chips from the grocery bag and put it on the table, with that feel-free-to-open-and-eat look. Time for more layers to come off with the help of chips and some pop I pulled out of the fridge. My mom was obviously more mature than Greg and I combined. She was sincerely warm in the way she talked and offered him the freedom to make this kitchen his own.

More layers were being peeled off, yes, but the anger inside me was taking longer to calm down than his nervousness. I had to keep telling myself how awkward this must all be for him. BUT STILL!

My brother David came in the house, probably sensing the chip bag was open. Greg seemed a lot more comfortable when meeting David, perhaps because the two of them were pretty much the same age. After a quick handshake, David grabbed a handful of chips and, of course, asked, "So how was your flight?" and then headed out to wherever his next adventure was, either to his job or to hang out with a friend. David did not live at home anymore. Instead, he was renting someplace close by with a friend, but he stopped in often to do a little staring into the fridge to see if there was anything to eat, just as we all frequently did while growing up.

List

Pick him up – check

Look like I know it's gonna work out – check

Feel awkward when it's time to say goodnight – check

That last one wasn't really on my list for the day, but I knew it would happen.

Okay, now what? It's time to say goodnight. By this point he had shared a little more with my parents about his family back in California, along with more talking just between the two of us. There was this sense in the air to wait for the next day to do more in-depth chit-chat about what would be our new life: wedding details, finding a job, and starting a family. Or, using just one word, reality. I feel I should mention that, as evening drew near and he was relaxing a bit more, he did utter one really simple "Hi, baby," while looking at my tummy.

Saying goodnight that night was weird. Do we act like we're happily engaged? Say lots of cute things and sound like we were meant for each other and give one big smooch goodnight? Or do we just say, "See ya tomorrow," and give each other a high five? None of these. Just a warm hug with a "See ya in the morning," from me, and a sweet, "It was nice meeting your family. Goodnight," from him.

And off I went to my room by myself. The only thing in the entire world I wanted was my pillow. Sure, my future husband was just a few steps down the hall in David's old room. But all I wanted was for it to be dark in my room, away from the world, and a miracle that somehow my pillow could take all my thoughts away. *He's here. He is nice and can be fun to be around, but did he really think he could hide behind me? Glad he and David sort of hit it off, but still, I can't believe I'm going to marry him. Do I really have to wake up in the morning?*

Finally, after an extra-long time thinking all this and after asking God, again, to please help me, my pillow finally heard "zzzzzzzz."

CHAPTER 5
Dream On, Marianne

Okay, it's real. He's here. It's happening. No more waking up to only my concerns and doing what I feel like doing. Something's just not right in how all this is working out. Come on, Me, get up... In a few minutes.

By now I was used to the fact that I'd soon be a mom and would be caring for, with tons of help all around me, an adorable baby. But the fact that I'd have a man with me from now on I'd soon call my husband? Sorry. I wasn't used to that fact yet and didn't really feel like jumping out of bed that morning.

I should tell you a bit more how I was feeling. I don't want it to sound like I was totally disgusted with Greg. After all, we hit it off in California, and he seemed to have a great personality. Not perfect, but still sweet and kind. So I don't want it to sound like I couldn't stand him and that I totally dreaded starting this day. I was just feeling that this day would begin the rest of my life, or however long God had in mind, with this man. I guess I still had some feelings for him and still believed God could be using all this to save him. Plus, he *was* handsome. But still, I knew I didn't love him and didn't really feel too comfortable with all that was about to happen.

Okay, here I go.

I don't remember if we first saw each other that morning downstairs in the kitchen or if he walked in as I was sitting on the couch talking with my mom as she sat on the carpeted floor, smoking in front of that empty fireplace. Did my mom make us her great scrambled egg breakfast or did I just grab my own cereal? I don't know. All I remember is that the day of getting comfortable and having mostly lighthearted talk was over. Oh, one thing I do remember. He wanted coffee. No comment.

The first full day of discussing our wedding, making decisions, and facing reality was here. But I do remember one of the first things he did that day. He gave me a sweet good-morning kiss on my cheek and then, putting his hand on my tummy, said, "Good morning, little baby in there." It was kind of cute.

What was on top of the to-do list had to be done that day. Get the legal requirements needed to be married, which led us to an office to apply for the marriage license. No longer were we just talking about tying the knot. We needed to sign the paper which allowed us to get the marriage certificate that we would fill out after we said the I dos.

Okay, pen, here I go. I began filling that part out, feeling God must have been approving it, since I was right then and there signing my name and He was in control of my life. Marianne Can't-Believe-I'm-Signing-This Houstoun. It was sort of weird when it was Greg's turn to sign. He had a slight look of discomfort on his face, but I'm sure my face must have shown that too. After all, it wouldn't be long until we both signed more papers stating that we would have tied the knot.

It's now Sunday. The first Sunday he's in town and the first Sunday I get to take him to, no longer just my church, but *our* church. It's not like he was jumping to go, but still very willing to follow my rule: go to church. Through all of this, I knew church was a necessity. I learned that was a must from not thinking that way in California.

"It's just a fact," I said. "You and I have to get settled in going to church, this week and next week and the next."

I made sure I told him as many positive things about the church as I could. After all, I didn't want him hiding behind my back there when I introduced him to my friends.

By this point I hadn't yet told him how I believed he wasn't a true Christian. I wasn't comfortable saying things like that. After all, if he wasn't saved but thought he was, I felt the preaching up on the pulpit could explain it better than me. The only spiritual thing we talked about, because of what happened, was God's view on abortion, and I knew Greg needed more, lots more.

Being that Emmanuel was a smaller church, by now everyone there knew our story. I'm sure they all were curious what this guy looked like whom I was about to marry. Sure, I was nervous what they would think, but my thoughts were more on what Pastor Mark would think.

We pulled into the parking lot, got out of the car, and I could tell Greg was nervous. I was too. I mean, trying to look happy and in love wasn't the easiest look to make. While walking inside we both smiled, and the people there smiled back at us. The most anyone said then, since the piano was being played as others were coming in to sit down, was, "So this is your fiancé. Glad to meet you." I was glad there wasn't time for any in-depth discussions.

Will he like it here? Will the other ladies think he's cute? How should I introduce him? What are people thinking? Where should we sit? There, I liked that last question the most.

We wound up sitting toward the front on the left. I don't know what I was thinking! Why have everyone else behind us? No one could avoid seeing me and wonder who the guy was by my side! Oh, well. Too late to change seats now.

So there we were. Others were still walking in while the pianist played a nice, calm hymn. I could tell Greg was pretty comfortable because he had his arm behind me. Ahh, how sweet. I then turned my head, looking behind his head to take a quick glimpse at those behind us.

Who can see us up here? Who's looking? One last look. *I need to stop looking behind us.* That last look, however, proved something right then and there. Love at first sight is possible.

As I looked, in walked this gorgeous man I had never seen

before. Slow motion goes into effect once again. This handsome man, about my age, had just walked in holding a Bible and looking around for a place to sit. I froze. I stared. I stared some more. But I caught myself and shook my head.

Come on, Marianne, think. Think! You're getting married in a few weeks. Ignore that man. It's too late. Too late to find someone else. But man, he's cute! No. Face reality and keep facing forward.

I then felt the sadness sink deep, deep inside. Sadness for reality. Great. Our first church service starts and I'm sitting with the man I'll be marrying, feeling down in the dumps, dwelling on the fact that I've missed out on the excitement of feeling all the God-given joy of falling in love with a fellow believer, which would by far get more of God's blessings.

No, stop thinking of this love at first sight. You're marrying Greg in a few weeks. Face it. No one else. He'll change. He'll change. You'll love him someday... maybe.

The church service was over, and my mind was fried as the last hymn came to an end. The sounds of people standing up had begun. *Why can't this be one of the churches where everyone just leaves?* Only a fraction of the sixty or so attenders, adults and children combined, leave right after the service. Most everyone stays and visits with one another. I thought I'd want to do that today too, but that was before seeing that new man there. The longer we stayed, the more I saw that guy and the more I wished I wasn't getting married. I couldn't be rude, however, and ignore the people who were coming over to meet Greg.

"You must be Greg. Glad to meet you," or "Please let us know how we can help you get ready for the wedding." So nice. And, thankfully, Greg came across very nice as well. No big discussions, of course. Or maybe they did have them and I just wasn't paying much attention because one eye was looking at who was talking to us while the other, you guessed it, was looking for that other man. I didn't want to meet him; don't think that at all. Looking at him was enough. But life is never easy, for he was right in between where I was standing and the door I was trying to get to. Sure enough, someone led us over to meet this man who had just started visiting the church.

"Chris, this is Marianne and Greg. You two, this is Chris Petersen."

"Hello," Chris said. Even his voice was cute.

A few very short facts of our upcoming wedding were shared, and then he told us what got him coming to Emmanuel in the first place. I found out that when I'd taken off to California, God had guided Chris to Himself through a Bible study that wasn't connected with Emmanuel. That had sparked a desire to know more about God, and that spark caused him to listen to someone suggest going to Emmanuel. When he was sharing all that with us, I wanted to just gaze at him while, at the same time, feeling the need to leave as soon as possible. Love at first sight was messing me up.

"Well, it was nice meeting you, but we must be off," I said after pondering what I should say to escape.

Before we got to my car, we had a quick talk with Pastor Mark, setting a time and place for the three of us to meet and talk about our getting married. We needed more than just one or two times of simple 'Hello, how are you' talks at church. Pastor Mark knew about our plans, but at this point had not given the hundred percent yes to say 'I now pronounce you man and wife.' The time and place to meet in a few days was set. Back to the house.

It was impossible for me not to think about that man named Chris. For the rest of that day I just day-dreamed off and on while thinking many 'what-ifs.'

What if I met Chris without Greg there? What if I wasn't pregnant? I wonder if Chris has anyone he's serious with? Oh, he probably does. Chris sure talks nice. I like the name 'Chris.'

My pillow that night was, I'm sure, relieved to feel a few refreshing moments as it noticed thoughts of this new man. But I'm also sure my pillow was sensing those normal, heavy thoughts too. Seeing that man had me wishing over and over again that I could marry the first man I would truly fall in love with. Sad to admit that hope was dead.

Only a day or two later we met with Pastor Mark for a simple dessert at a simple sit-down restaurant for a simple first talk. It wasn't a big planned discussion to cover the ninety-nine things that pastors want to cover before marrying a couple. Nope. It was for him to hear the story about our relationship and to get a feel for who Greg was. Pastor Mark was very warm and friendly, yet serious. I could tell he cared for me by trying to find out as much as possible about this man I was to marry.

He did state that just because the wedding was pretty much planned to happen soon, he couldn't right then and there say he was fully behind it all and felt we should meet and talk a few more times. Greg and I could understand, and I respected Mark's thoughts very much. Actually, I was sort of relieved with his idea to wait.

Another reason to wait was the sad fact that Brenda, my sister's daughter, had only a few more days to live. I couldn't avoid thinking about that even with all the other stuff I had to deal with. A beautiful little girl. Her battle to live made it even harder for us to be all gung-ho for the wedding. I wanted to help my sister out, so holding the wedding off a few weeks helped me do just that.

Once again, I need to say that I don't remember all that went on in that talk with Pastor Mark as we ate pie. I do remember, though, that he acted very responsible in guiding me, one of his sheep. Keep in mind, however, that at that time I felt stronger in following what I thought was right and not so much what my pastor, or scripture, was saying. I felt I should get married even if Greg wasn't saved. I had told Pastor Mark from the very start that I was pretty convinced Greg wasn't saved, but since he was my future child's father, that I should marry him. The clear fact that scripture says a believer is not to be unequally yoked with an unbeliever wasn't, at that time, something I knew much about. Perhaps Pastor Mark should have been a bit bolder, strongly advising me to not marry Greg. Or, most likely, I just let my emotions and ignorance take control. *He just isn't fully understanding all I'm going through.*

After a while, we all knew it was time to put our first time getting together to an end, agreeing to plan a day early next week to talk more. I was so thankful the talk went well. Between these two men, there was no argument, no big discussion about believers marrying unbelievers, and it even ended with smiles and a handshake. I can picture it all now, as we left the restaurant.

Well, I'm glad that's over. I hope Pastor Mark noticed something positive about Greg and can understand why I feel marrying him is right. Perhaps it went so great that I'll even stop thinking about that new guy at church. Heck, it might even be good I'm going to marry Greg.

As we walked to the car, I began to feel pretty positive. Besides that wedding dress I got and the fact that he liked coffee, things were starting to look better.

So, you might be wondering how Greg and I were getting along physically at this point. It's sort of like asking how does one feel while slowly wading into a cold swimming pool. At first it's uncomfortable and you want to get out, but as a minute or two goes by, it's not so bad. You get used to it, right? You slowly walk in deeper and deeper. Well, it sort of got to be like that with me around Greg. At first, man, was I cold with him and wanted to turn around and escape it all. But as days went by, I got used to Greg and his personality and could see why I fell for him in the first place. We had gotten used to the fact that we'd soon be parents, and no one was telling me I was doing anything wrong in marrying him. I then began to feel more relaxed about it all and, sad to say, allowed too much physical contact to start up again. Now sure, my guilt was there, but I convinced myself with that popular thinking, "Well, since we're getting married soon, then doing a bit more than a kiss here and there is okay." God knew my heart, though. He knew that, deep inside, I knew better than to play around at all. My thoughts were so confused about so much at that point, and I just wanted to believe anything was okay. *After all, all things will be fine to do in a few weeks.*

Back to life. Another day or two went by. More trying hard to only see the positive out of it all. Him looking for a job, me still not wanting to see that dress hanging up in my closet, and both of us getting used to the fact that in a few weeks we'd most likely be husband and wife. I still believe God gave His okay because, after all, it was happening.

On one of those days Brenda passed away. So much sadness. My sister and her husband had six children total. Brenda was their fifth. The funeral was the first time in years almost all of my family was together. That meant it was the first opportunity for Greg to see most of them. It was actually good, in a way, for all to meet before the wedding that was to occur very soon.

Chapter 6
The Hot Cocoa Explosion

He's all relaxed around my family – check

Marriage license – check

Simple wedding planning done – check

Go to church – check

Try to believe love at first sight isn't real – check

Pastoral talk – check

Getting used to him patting my tummy every morning, saying "good morning, baby" – no, but I'll still say check.

So now to do what was next on the list. Spend a good batch of time with my two best friends, Willma and Eyde.

"How about we all go catch our old high school's homecoming football game?" one of the twins suggested.

"Sounds perfect! None of us have been there for a while, and it's a good open area with lots to look at. It's cheap too. Let's go," responded me, Marianne Find-A-Way-To-Get-Them-To-Know-Greg Houstoun.

Eyde and Willma had known that my feelings were going up and down that last month, so I knew they weren't going just to watch football. Nope, they wanted to check out this guy I was going to marry in a few weeks.

"Hi, Greg. Glad to finally meet you," Eyde said, the first of many friendly, simple, and sweet comments among us as I drove all four of us to the game.

It was kind of weird driving up to my old high school. Two

years before was the beginning of my senior year, playing in that same marching band on that same field. Oh, what I would have given to make it two years earlier, only worrying if my frozen fingers, playing my saxophone, would hit the right notes.

It was a rather windy October evening, and the sun was beginning to set. We were glad we had our coats on, zipped all the way up. I was quite glad, while walking up those steps, that I had on my thick coat to hide any proof I was a little over two months' pregnant. We quickly sat down out of the wind as the game started.

It was only about fifteen minutes that we all chatted back and forth while watching the game before I could tell Greg was trying to impress Willma and Eyde. I can't exactly describe it, but, because of a certain thing, he started to show a side of himself I didn't know was there. That thing? Hot cocoa. As soon as one of us saw someone carrying a cup, a couple of us exclaimed, "Oh, that looks delicious!"

Instantly Greg said, "Here, let me go get all of us some."

How sweet of him. "Sure! Sounds perfect! As long as it's not coffee," I said.

"Sure, thanks," Willma replied.

But Eyde? Eyde was the oddball who said, "No. I'm fine. Thanks, though." She either didn't want it or was being nice, figuring he couldn't carry a total of four drinks with two hands.

Greg, however, insisted. "I'll get you some too, Eyde."

"No, you don't have to," Eyde matter-of-factly responded.

"No, I want to."

Okay, Greg, that's enough. Willma and I looked at each other.

But no! Greg insisted, with an I'm-offering-so-you-accept-or-else look on his face, while staring straight into her eyes. "I'm getting you some."

Um, Greg, shut up. I couldn't help but start to feel that those around us were noticing some friction forming.

Back and forth, "No, you won't." "Yes, I will," a few too many times.

Why can't he just HUSH? This is getting ridiculous!

The uneasiness and embarrassment were growing. He stood up to leave, squeezing in front of others who were sitting next to us as he headed toward the stairs.

Okay, now what? Willma and I looked at each other, then at Eyde, who showed a bit of steam blustering out of her ears.

"Eyde, I'm sorry. I don't know why he's forcing you to take some. Maybe he just wants you to think he's a good guy."

But anything I said she just let go in one ear as steam flew out the other. Back comes Greg, carefully holding three cups of hot cocoa.

"Thank you," Willma and I quickly said, hoping that's exactly what Eyde would say. But no.

"I *told* you I don't want any," she firmly said.

"Here, take it. I got it for you." Of course you know who said that.

The war had begun. *Why? Why did he get one for her? Does he have a few screws missing?* Questioning looks increased on the faces of the people around us. We could tell there was no way to calm this war.

"I'VE HAD IT!" she hollered while standing up, managing to get over to the stairs and then walking down. He, however, was determined not to lose and began following her. Willma and I were shocked this was happening and had confused looks on our faces. We got up, making sure we grabbed anything else we brought in. Something told us we weren't coming back.

So there we were in a line. Eyde first, Greg six feet behind her, and Willma and me, side by side, about six feet behind him, all walking swiftly away from everyone else.

"Greg! Stop it!" Eyde kept saying, "I don't want it!" At the same time Greg was repeating, "You'll take it! You'll take it!"

Eyde finally stopped and turned around, with the angriest look on her face.

"I. DON'T. WANT. ANY!"

He stopped walking and held the cup closer to her face. "Drink!"

"No!"

"Yes!"

"NO!"

Back and forth, back and forth, holding it up to her mouth as her head turned left and right. That hot cocoa, obviously not so hot anymore, sort of splashed around and some got on her coat.

Um, excuse me, but am I missing something? Didn't we come here to watch a football game, not see two adults get angry over hot cocoa? I guess I was wrong.

Willma and I, looking at each other, both said, "I guess we're going now."

We made our way to the car. Two faces were red hot with anger, cold cocoa on the face of one, while the other two who were watching all this were stunned at what just happened. No one said anything. Obviously the two who were steaming didn't sit next to each other during that silent ride back home.

As soon as we parked outside my house, Eyde got out, slammed the door, and started marching down to her house. Willma, with her I'm-sorry-it-happened look, said something like "I guess we're walking home now."

You'd think I'd have more to say on all I was feeling that night and the next day, but something occurred a few days later that makes the cocoa fight, and the few days that followed, seem like a nice walk in the park.

CHAPTER 7
You're WHAT?

It was about four or five days before the wedding and I was talking with my mom, probably about last-minute wedding details, while Greg was watching TV in the rec-room.

Ring, ring. Ring, ring I heard just an arm's length away.

"I'll get it, Mom," I said. "Hello. Oh, hi, Susan. I'm fine." It was Greg's mom. Twenty-million thoughts instantly formed. *What's she calling about? Is something wrong? Is she saying they now plan to come to the wedding? Is she offering to pay for a better wedding dress?* Whatever it was about, I wanted to be on the phone in my room.

My mom could tell I was suddenly nervous and let me know she'd hang up the kitchen phone after I got on the one in my bedroom.

"Okay, Mom, got it," I said loudly from my room.

Now it was just Susan and me.

"Hello, Marianne."

Notice it was 'Hello' and not just a simple 'Hi.' On she went. "I needed to call and tell you something. Have you been wondering why Greg's dad and I haven't been part of our own son's wedding?"

"Well, since you asked, yes. But I just assumed it was too soon of a wedding, and with you all in California..."

I don't know if anyone reading has noticed, but I haven't added his parents at all into this story. Why? Greg just gave some simple excuse that they weren't able to be part of the wedding and left it at that. I guess I didn't want to know why and didn't force more info out of him. I was told they were giving the okay, with love and support for whatever we decided, and just weren't able to make it.

"Marianne, there is a... well, you see, there's a..."

Yes. Yes, keep going.

"...there's a legal reason why he shouldn't be marrying you."

"WHAT?" I couldn't hold back. "I don't get it. What do you mean, 'legal reason'? What we are doing is all legal. We went into the place, signed all this stuff. What in the world do you mean, not legal?"

"Legally, right now, he cannot get married. I've been hoping he would have told you by now, but I can see he hasn't. I felt I should call you."

"But what do you mean he can't legally marry me now? What's illegal about it?" I asked with an obviously stunned look on my face that no one was around to see. I still remember how I was holding the phone while standing next to my little desk, looking at the little jewelry box holding those brand-spankin'-new earrings. One of those phone calls that stands out, by far, as one I'll never forget.

"Marianne, Greg cannot legally marry you, but he needs to explain it."

"What? How... wha... WHAT? Why can't you tell me?"

Talk about something totally unexpected happening! Hearing that the man I'm to marry in a few days is doing something legally wrong wasn't really on my day's expectation list.

"Sorry, Marianne, that I had to bring it to you this way, but I knew you needed to know."

A few seconds went by. I was sort of acting like Greg did to me when I called him and he didn't talk. Silence.

"Marianne? Are you there?"

"Yes. Yes, I'm here. But what did—"

"I don't feel right giving you all the details about this. I just know someone needed to tell you something. Greg needs to tell you the rest. I'm sorry, Marianne."

I don't remember how that talk ended. I just know it felt like my life was maybe, just maybe, turning into a soap opera. I was so shocked with that new fact that nothing else said really mattered. I'm sure it didn't end with 'Have a good day.'

Now what? What does one do after learning they were about to get married illegally? I didn't know what to think as I stood all alone in my room, looking at my pillow, wishing I could just toss my thoughts on it. I walked out of my room.

Mom. I need my mom! Thankfully, as I left my room, Mom was at her bedroom door with the most curious look on her face.

"What's going on?" she slowly asked.

I responded very quickly by pointing into her room. She and I went in and I shut the door.

"Mom, Greg's mom just told me there is a legal reason why we can't get married!"

"WHAT?" she burst out.

I had to say 'shhh' as I put my pointer finger over my mouth, but only for her to say it again as a loud whisper. "What?"

I then told her all Greg's mom had told me.

"Now! Marianne, you need to go find out NOW!" she told me, with a bit of hot steam slowly forming around her graying hair.

Only half a second went by before I felt brave enough to march into his room. He wasn't there. Where was he? *Oh, that's right. He's in the TV room.* I'm sure he sensed something was up when he heard someone pounding down the stairs. I walked into the TV room to find him sitting on the recliner, reading something.

"Greg, your mom just called," I said with not a hint of relaxation in my tone, "and she said there is a legal reason why we can't get married. Explain, please."

His nonchalant look instantly did a hundred-and-eighty-degree turn into a terrified, I'm-gonna-die look. It confirmed he'd been hiding something. I was gracious and allowed him twenty millionths of a second to start talking. Nothing said except what his facial expression had to say: I'm dead.

I barked two demanding words. "Tell me!"

He quietly replied with two excruciating words. "I'm married."

An official soap opera had begun. I froze. Silence for a few very long seconds. "You're married," said as a fact. "You're married?" asked as a question. The only two words I could come up with at that point. "You're mar..."

He instantly started talking a mile a minute. "Yes, Marianne. I've been too scared to tell you all along about—"

"You're married?"

He then began to explain.

"You see, after high school, I was in the Army."

"The Army," I repeated. Suddenly I started hearing things about him I never would have imagined.

"I was sent to Europe, met a lady who lived there, fell in love, and got married. When the time I had to serve there was over, she and I agreed we didn't want to stay together. I then came back home to California, but she stayed there."

"So, let's see if I've got this right. You got married there but came back home to live with your mom and dad while she stayed in Europe." I couldn't believe I was saying this, "And you both just stayed married to each other. Then what?"

"Shortly after I got home is when I started working where you and I met. Obviously you know the rest."

Now it all made sense. All along I felt I wasn't hearing much about his life from when he graduated high school to when I met him. I never really asked. I just figured he didn't have a lot to say. Boy, was I wrong. It then made total sense to me why he had that certain look on his face as he signed that pre-marriage paper a few weeks before.

He continued. "So she stayed there, I came home, and we just avoided what we should have done: get a divorce. Then I met you, we got our relationship going, you moved home, then told me you're pregnant, and it was then I filed for divorce."

"Filed for divorce." I'm good at stating facts now. "How long until you are—"

"Divorced? About five-and-a-half months."

"I cannot believe this. I just cannot believe this," I said, slowly shaking my head while walking back and forth in the TV room. "I *cannot* believe this."

Time now for the question of a lifetime. "Why didn't you **tell** me?" making the word 'tell' stand out a little more than the rest.

His answer—make sure you're sitting down as you read this—"I loved you too much to tell you."

WHAT? He loved me too much? He loved me too much to tell me I was getting illegally married to him? Sorry, but the second I heard that proved to me he was far from being mature and didn't understand at all what true love was supposed to be. I needed to leave.

"I'll be right back. You stay here," I said while thinking a record-breaking amount of questions that could be made from the TV room to Mom's room.

What do I do now? Who do I tell? When do I tell? Do I still marry him? What about this baby? And, WHY IN THE WORLD DID GOD DO THIS TO ME?

As I was leaving the room, my sister Kelly came in the house and was close to that door, sensing, from the look on my face, that something was up. Seeing Greg sitting on that recliner, she couldn't help but feel a need to be polite and so passed a little hello to him. I'm sure you can imagine how uncomfortable he was needing to instantly fake some relaxing chit-chatting.

My mom looked like she was about to explode with curiosity as I got into her room.

"Whatdidhesay?" sounding as if it were all one word.

"Mom." I paused a little while shaking my head back and forth. *I can't believe this. I CANNOT believe this.* "Mom, you're not going to believe this. He's married."

I'll never forget what she started doing as I began telling the story. No words were needed, because her look said it all. Her fists were clenching like they were ready to punch something, while her eyes were getting bigger as a ferocious face was forming. I was pretty much done talking when she decided to copy me and pound down those stairs. I went right behind her, not knowing what to expect as she growled, with her top teeth firmly pushing on her lower teeth, "Where. Is. He?" she said to herself, knowing exactly where he was.

Kelly was there talking to Greg when Mom interrupted, but not with words. King Kong walked right over to the recliner Greg was reclining in, pounded her foot on the stretched-out end where his feet were, and forcefully pushed it down, causing the chair, and Greg, to quickly pop up straight. No sign of a calm, self-controlled adult woman to be found in our house that afternoon. Having dealt with her granddaughter's funeral about a week prior to this, plus tons of thoughts toward this wedding, allowed her to turn in her do-whatever-you-feel-like ticket.

"Explain. Explain why you did this! Explain why you were about to marry my daughter, knowing you are already married!"

Of course, anything he tried to say disintegrated after entering Mom's ears. My sister couldn't believe what she was hearing, causing her head to steam as well. Greg was trying to explain why it was hard for him to tell us, but, no matter what he said, our compassion meter was at zero.

"Look at my daughter," Mom barked while pointing to me. "Look what you're putting her through," as tears poured down my face. I can still picture that whole scene. My mom and sister's anger showed love to me, weird as that may sound, and I sure needed that right then.

Whirlpools of thoughts kept churning through my head. Though controlling my crying was impossible with all this going on, I found myself becoming somewhat numb. I was sort of going into my own little world. I didn't know what to think with this loud hollering all around me. I felt like I was turning into an invisible cloud looking down at this loud commotion that was all about me. All about me being pregnant. All about me and how big of a fool I was that one night in California. All those thoughts added a heavy weight to my tears.

I don't remember how that—what shall I call it—'conversation' ended, but somehow I wound up on my pillow wishing it had arms to pat me on the back and say "there, there. I'm here." I'm sure it got a bit tired of hearing my *"Why? Why, God? Why?"* thoughts over and over and over again. The only reason I know I somehow fell asleep is because the next morning I somehow woke up. It was one of these mornings when the list of what to think about doesn't really seem to start as fast as most mornings. But then, sure enough, after thirty seconds or so it did. It felt like these two words that finally worked their way back weighed eighty pounds. HE'S MARRIED.

Now what? I knew somehow I had to get up and go start this day, but the who, what, where, when, how, and why list kept me in bed for as long as it could. I'm sure my pillow also wanted to punch Greg the more it felt all my thoughts.

Who – Whom do I talk to first?

What – What do I say to whomever I talk to first?

Where – Where will I cry next?

When – When should I decide if, after the divorce, I will or will not marry Greg?

How – How do I tell people about all this?

And last but not least:

Why – Why did God allow this to happen?

As I lay there waiting for answers, none popped up. I finally told myself I needed to control my emotions, if possible. I needed to get up and face reality, but boy, I sure didn't want to. Very briefly the night before Greg and I had tossed around a few ideas of what our options were.

1) Go our separate ways as he pays child support.

2) After his divorce is finalized, get married and live happily ever after.

3) Lock him on a Metro bus to Mars. I'd even pay.

(I was sure this would have been my mom's choice, by far.)

Not hearing the sounds of anyone else getting up, I did the last thing I felt like doing and got out of bed. Knowing Greg probably felt like staying in bed for the rest of his life, I was pretty darn sure I wouldn't see him as I, very quietly this time, walked downstairs. I sort of pictured my mom having coffee ready to offer Greg that would explode once sipped, but no. She was calmly smoking in front of that empty fireplace, coffee by her side. I could tell from the ashtray that she had smoked quite a bit more than normal that morning. I sat on the couch as usual, yet a little more numb, with no 'good-morning' words to be found. We stayed quiet for a minute.

"How are you feeling?" she asked me while tapping her cigarette into the fireplace. We then started talking about the night before, and she apologized for all the arguing.

"Mom, no need to apologize. I totally understand."

"What do you think you should do?" she asked. "I just want you to know that you are free to stay here with your baby, but without him, as long as you want. Please don't feel like you have to still marry him." She pretty much left it at that. She knew she didn't need to give many of her own opinions. After last night, it was pretty obvious what they were.

The more I sat there and the more I thought, the more distance I felt from any right answer. As a little time went by, it dawned on me that word needed to get out that the wedding was canceled. I won't even get into how hard it was for me to think of who and how to tell.

"Oh, Mom, why does telling people things have to be so hard?" My mom and I decided who would call whom and what we'd say.

Oh, no, someone was now walking down the stairs. Reality. Greg was coming down. There were some obvious signs among us that the fewer words, the better. Honestly, I don't recall what we said when we finally saw each other that morning. My mom's despising look began to form while staring into the empty fireplace. At least her mouth didn't say anything and steam wasn't coming out of her ears. Greg and I just didn't know what to say to each other. 'Good morning' sure didn't feel right. He knew not to say his normal "Good morning, little baby" or pat my tummy. "What's for breakfast?" wouldn't have been a great choice either. Not one of us went out of our way to talk to each other. I stayed put; Mom stayed put. Greg went into the kitchen and got his own something to eat and then went back to his room. Too soon to face reality.

I did make a few phone calls. Willma had tried hard to stay positive with all that had gone on before this, and again, gave her support to me. Pastor Mark, too, was so kind. No big discussion about it all, but I could tell he truly cared. I just told him in the simplest form what had happened.

"I'm so sorry, Marianne," he said with all sincerity. "I'll take care of everything on this end, and we'll sure be praying for you." He also knew, at that point, the fewer words, the better.

Now I'll be honest. When I saw that wedding dress hanging in my closet, I definitely didn't have a frown on my face. *Good! I don't have to WEAR that now.* That smile sure was needed. But once I turned around, I quickly got back to that sober feeling. *Now what?*

The atmosphere in our house was so uncomfortable that day. Greg kept saying how sorry he was, but that was when he wasn't in his own room. He'd rather be there than see my mom's face, fearing she'd like to punch him if he was within a twenty-yard radius. It did help knowing my dad would be gone to work all day. I'll admit, I, too, was in my own room, just lying down, wishing my pillow and I could escape life.

As hours went by, the little baby inside was, I felt, the one in charge. The baby. My baby. He or she was the reason behind all that was going on. I started feeling that what would be best for the baby comes first. What's best for the baby is what I would need to follow. But, what *is* best for the baby? I so strongly wanted my first baby to have as normal a life as possible, and having a father and mother from the start would make that happen. After all, wouldn't God want that? And if I felt strongly about that, then God would bless that attempt. Right? Keeping Greg in the story was, then, starting to sink in.

By the end of that first day, a day full of me hearing, "Marianne, let me know if I can get you anything," or "Any thoughts on what you will do?" from family, and, of course, "Please forgive me, Marianne," from you know who, I didn't tell anyone what my thoughts were until the next day.

"But Mom, I feel strongly about giving Greg another chance, or at least not saying it's a hundred percent over," I said that next morning by the fireplace. "He messed up with what happened, but this baby needs its father. Greg wants to, and I should at least give him a chance."

My mom didn't like my decision to not call the whole thing off, but she knew she couldn't change my mind. Dad and Kelly weren't too gung-ho with my decision either, but were more agreeable as long as he didn't stay at our house. Of course I agreed to that, but just not forcing him back to California right then, which would totally erase him from me and from our baby's life. My heart and mind were coming to the simple realization that love or no love, the baby was to come first. Greg agreed. Heck, he knew best *not* to disagree with me about anything those first few days after that TV-room experience. My mom just hoped, by telling me over and over and over again that I could stay with her and Dad for however long I wanted, that she would somehow convince me to send him back to California.

Remember how I felt rather numb that evening the truth was discovered? I remained that way with each passing day. I was extremely fried from all my thoughts going up and down and simply wanted to stop it all, somehow. Even the way I talked was neutral sounding. No real sad or happy tone of voice. As a few days went by, I was feeling more set in my decision to stick it out and stay with Greg. *We'll get married when the divorce is finalized. Feels easy enough. That's all. I'm sick of thinking.* I left it at that. I hadn't really sought others' advice, wise or unwise, and just leaned on what I was thinking God wanted me to think. Thus, I felt frozen inside and wanted to stick with some plan and then stop thinking. *I'm just gonna do what's best for the baby. I'm tired of thinking what's best for me.*

No big announcement was made, but Greg and I felt comfortable enough to plan for him to stay in town, get a job, find a cheap apartment, and just see what happens.

Now don't you dare think we started acting like we were the sweetest engaged couple in the world. No. I'm sure if anyone saw us, they'd just think we were brother and sister. No affection whatsoever, and you can bet I wasn't missing that.

I remember those first few nights on my pillow, when going to bed was my favorite time and place. My life, and all I had to face, was nowhere to be found. No faces to look at. No asking or answering questions. No hearing the sound of him coming down the stairs. The only sad part about going to bed was knowing it was going to come to an end once the new morning hit. Tears each night, yes, but my pillow was right there, getting used to that while hearing my 'why' and 'what-if' thoughts.

Why can't all this be just some kind of dream? Why can't I just go to sleep, wake up, and start life all over again with none of this to face? What if he did go back to California? What if the baby has some serious problem? What if Greg and I end up fighting a lot? What if I want to go back to college? And, of course, *Why, God?*

CHAPTER 8
The Walk

Ring, ring. Ring, ring.

"Marianne, it's for you," Mom said, handing me the phone.

"Oh, sure. Yeah, I'll be ready," I said to the person on the other end. Huge grin on my face. "Mom, Eyde and Willma are bored and want to walk over, and then the three of us will go do something."

Since they lived just a few houses down, I knew they'd be at my house any minute. I also knew I needed some fresh air and time with dear friends on that warm, sunny day. I was so tired, for about two days now, with everyone tiptoeing about with all that tension floating through the air. Greg, for the most part, stayed in his room. I had not gone to church since the blow up, so hadn't seen refreshing faces for days. Getting out was perfect, just what the doctor ordered. Through Greg's bedroom door I told him I would be gone for a bit, knowing he would, even more so, just stay in that room reading the part in the newspaper with the title 'Now hiring.'

A hot day. Shorts, tank top, and flip flops were a must. When they came to the door, each of them was carrying a tall cup filled with ice water.

"What? Eyde? You mean you didn't bring hot cocoa?" I had to say. We all laughed.

"Hey, ready for a walk?" one asked.

"Sure. Let me go get something to drink too."

Then off we went. A breath of fresh air, and, oh, how I needed that. Very lighthearted chit-chat as we began walking out of our dead-end street, soaking up that beautiful sunshine. We were only a few houses down the street when Eyde and Willma looked at each other. I saw a rather odd look pass between them.

"You want to know the real reason we wanted to see you?" asked Eyde.

Willma then continued, "Yeah. We need to talk to you about something."

"Um, what's this all about?" I asked while looking back and forth to each.

Eyde, with an unforgettably serious look on her face, said, "Marianne, you are *not* marrying Greg and he is to go back to California."

Willma quickly added, "And I totally agree."

Those two sentences started the longest walk I had ever taken, yet in many ways it seemed like the shortest.

"Marianne, you told us that you know he's not a Christian, right?"

"Right."

"That alone is enough of a reason not to marry him. God doesn't want you to. He has it in the Bible that a believer is not to marry an unbeliever. Now, if you need more reasons not to marry, I have more."

"I know that, but what if God wants to use me to save—" I tried to say, but got interrupted.

"Don't think about any 'what-ifs.' Another reason you're not marrying him is because you don't even love him! Right, Willma?"

"Yep! If you don't love him, don't marry him."

Willma was the perfect cheerleader while Eyde was the team quarterback.

This was the first time I was hearing something from a Christian perspective. Not just a "God's there to help you," but more direct instructions on what I should do. Man, was it gold to finally hear something like that. My family, lately, had been the only people

I'd been around. I assumed all the people from church were just wanting a few days to go by before bringing anything up. So having Eyde and Willma step in was like food to a starving soul.

"Marianne," Eyde went on, "God is your Father. He knows it's tough, but it will be tougher if you marry Greg. God doesn't want you to do that."

That talk soon covered many different areas of what God expects of true followers. God wants wives and children to have a God-fearing husband and father. The twins popped out verse after verse to support it all.

"Put God first, Marianne, and trust Him. He'll carry you, a single mom, with His loving arms, and guide you on what to do," Eyde said.

"That's right!" Miss Cheerleader added.

My mind was beginning to feel some refreshing sparks inside.

"Now, what are all the negative things you're feeling? Don't you see how they all connect to Greg? Take him away and just think how much lighter your weight will be."

"Yeah, don't you see?" you-know-who repeated.

They were so right. All the negative things I felt inside were related to him. Most had even been there before the big eruption happened. The more they talked, the more my refreshing sparks were becoming a downpour of peace and hope. Sadness and worry were dissolving. I started bursting out a list of why I knew he wasn't for me. Eyde and Willma, too, brought up quite a few things they noticed about him the first time they met. Eyde did have a few more, but we all know why.

We must have walked a couple miles, but it seemed like only a block with all the talking we were doing. Finally all three of us realized it was time to head back. As I turned around, it felt like I was turning my life around. Starting that walk I was low in spirit, confused, distraught, and scared of what the next days and months would bring. Nothing looked positive. I even felt God must have wanted me to suffer for my sin. But as Eyde, Willma, and I headed back, my middle name changed again. Marianne Overflowing-With-A-Refreshed-Spirit Houstoun.

It all made total sense now. I should not marry Greg because, one, he wasn't a true regenerated man, and two, I didn't love him. Now I didn't think Eyde was some sort of prophet or anything. Was it all of a sudden clear because of the way she said it, or perhaps Willma's cheerleading, "Yes, Marianne! You can do it"? No. It was because they were both right, and God used them to open my eyes. By the time we were almost back to my house, I knew that God truly loved me, using Eyde and Willma as His way to say, "Marianne, trust Me. Don't marry Greg."

We then talked about the support I'd have, some jobs I might be able to get, how they would love to help babysit and get info on financial aid, and on and on and on. I felt, with the many ideas we covered, that I *could* do it! I'll never forget the peace that was then covering me. What was nice, but kind of weird, was the absence of even thinking 'But I'll miss him.'

"Guys, I can't thank you enough," I said after Eyde gave a short prayer with Willma's strong "AMEN" following. Those two then began the short walk to their home, looking like they had just won the Super Bowl.

I opened my front door, feeling like I was now that quarterback, all ready to march right in and talk to Greg. I couldn't have cared less if the door exploded when I opened it. Nothing was going to stop me from finding him. Mom saw me walk in, and the look on her face indicated she knew something was up.

"Mom, where is he?" I asked with a serious yet calm voice.

"Uh, I think in his room. What are you—"

I was already halfway up. I don't know why I even asked. Of course that's where he was. There I went, marching up the stairs the same way I marched down the stairs a few days before. Once at the top, I saw him coming out of his room.

"Go in there," I calmly but firmly said while pointing to my room. I needed my room for strength.

Note: Thus far, during this one month he'd been in town, only a few moments really stood out. Him hiding behind my back as my mom opened that garage door; him forcing hot cocoa in Eyde's face that one windy night; and King Kong pushing down that recliner. And it would be impossible to forget that eye-opening walk and talk with Eyde and Willma I just shared. But, I think the top of that list now goes to the way he looked as I pointed to my room. He looked at me, realizing I wasn't so happy-go-lucky. He slowly went past me, going where I was pointing, walking backward while facing me.

Now try to picture this: he and I face-to-face, about three feet apart, him walking backward with a scared look as I'm slowly marching toward him. He was getting closer and closer to the wall, looking from left to right for somewhere to escape. His back finally hit the wall. While still looking at me, slowly but surely he started going down, knees poking out with his backside against the wall. As his rear end hit the floor, his look was as if he had just seen a ghost.

"Greg, there is something I need to tell you," I authoritatively said while looking down to him. "Greg, sorry, but we're done. You are getting a ticket and flying back to California, tomorrow if possible. No if, ands, or buts." *Oh, that felt good.*

I then explained how Eyde and Willma opened my eyes to what would be best for both of us. I gave a list of why I didn't want this relationship to continue. I knew he wouldn't understand all of my reasons, but felt he still needed to hear them.

"So I hope you can see it's just best if we end it all as soon as possible. I will have plenty of support, the baby will be surrounded with love, and, I'll be honest, the baby will have a much happier mom."

Are you wondering how he reacted? Greg just stayed quiet. As I stepped back a few feet, he began to stand up.

"Are you sure?" was his first response.

I could sense the weight lifting off his back. After all, how would you feel if that I-really-don't-like-you aroma was all you could smell?

"I see what you're saying," he said, "and it makes sense. You're right." A few repetitions of 'I'm sorry for all this,' were said before he left the room to check out airlines for the earliest flight.

There I was, all by myself in my room, wondering if that last hour was for real.

God, thank you. Thank you. THAAANK YOU! I then collapsed on my bed, my pillow soaking up my excitement. It must have thought, "Excuse me, but, um, is this the same Marianne who's been here these last three months? I like this new Winnipoops just a wee bit more."

Well, of course I had to tell someone. Down to the kitchen.

"Mom, guess what?" I asked while staring at her tell-me, tell-me look. "I called it off and he's, hopefully, flying back to California tomorrow."

Her true smile returned. I explained the walk and the talk. She may not have understood why I had these reasons either, but I'm sure for her it didn't really matter what the whys were. The final results were what counted. Everyone else I told that day also gave sighs of relief. Pretty much everyone I told from then on said something like, "Marianne, you will be so much happier as a mom with Greg out of the picture," or "I could tell he wasn't right for you," or "It was hard not telling you that you could do better." I honestly felt all of those things too, but the numbness or mummy-like way I had become kept those thoughts buried deep.

My pillow must have wondered what in the world had happened to me, because that night in bed, not a tear was shed. Regret-filled thoughts had disintegrated. But the main thing my pillow noticed was how that night was the first night in a few months I looked forward to the next day.

That next morning was the first day of my new life. That morning, getting on the couch, my mom had the biggest smile I'd seen lately.

"GOOD morning, Marianne."

"GOOD morning, Mom."

But there was one more thing that had to happen. I needed to take Greg to the airport. Thankfully he was able to get a flight for later that morning. Not much time to kill. Greg just stayed in his room as long as possible. The less time wondering what to say back and forth, the better. I'll never forget seeing him walk out of his room with that good old suitcase that never turned out to be ours.

"Goodbye, Mrs. Houstoun. Again, sorry," he said as we walked to the door.

"Bye."

Time to get in the car. The first few minutes were silent as my thoughts went all over the place. *Last time in the car with him. Pretty sure we won't see each other again. What do I tell the baby about his or her father? I'm so glad the airport is only five minutes away.* But my most mind-boggling thought was, how do I say goodbye?

Up to this point we hadn't made any decision about whether he would ever see the baby face-to-face or not. Pictures, sure, but in person? I think we both sensed that wouldn't happen and didn't really feel like talking about it.

What about child support, you ask. I told him in that falling-down, back-against-the-wall talk that I wasn't even going to try to collect money from him because I figured he couldn't pay for it anyway. Some may think that not getting child support from him was a dumb decision, but I just looked at him as a twenty-one-year-old, without a job, still living with his parents, so why force him to give me something he didn't have? The main reason, however, was because I wanted to totally start over. I believed that God would be right there, and, because of what had occurred the day before, God proved He already was.

As we made the last turn to the airport, we both knew we needed to say something.

"Sorry it all turned out this way," he said.

"Me too," I replied.

I knew I didn't want the last thing I would say to him to be some cruel statement, but I also knew I didn't want to say something common and meaningless either, like 'talk to ya later,' as if we'd be eternal chums.

"Don't worry," he said as we soon had to decide where to go with my car. "You can just drop me off here."

What? No sitting uncomfortably with each other inside the airport waiting for your plane to depart? Darn it. Something about me staying put, with my hands on the steering wheel, was what I preferred.

"I'll keep you posted if anything happens and I need to talk to you," I said, trying to seem mellow. I felt it wouldn't be nice to show on my face how happy I felt inside.

With so many cars around us, all he could do was get out, open the back door, quickly take his luggage out, come back to his side of the car and lean in one last time, saying, "Sorry again for all this. Goodbye."

"I know. Me too. Goodbye."

I watched him walk away, his back to me. The official it's-over feeling was such a relief. I'll never forget what that felt like. *Wow. I can't believe it. (Deep breath.) Last time here I picked him up, but now I just dropped him off. Oh, how weird this has been.*

As I left the airport and started back to the house, I savored, once again, the only thing I felt I needed to think about. Marianne Me-Myself-and-I Houstoun. But as I got home, turning to go up the driveway, Me-Myself-and-I changed. I felt even more joy inside as Me-Myself-and-I became God-My Baby-and-Me.

Once home, there was a new feeling in the air. You should have seen the look on my dad's face that night. His grin. Those eyes. He got his Winnipoops back. And there should be no surprise that, before I got in bed, I took that wedding dress off its hanger and put it in that big garbage can outside. If my pillow had an arm, we would have given each other high fives before I, ever-so-peacefully, fell asleep.

I must end this part of my story sharing that I realize I might have come across as some cruel, unsympathetic, selfish, pregnant nineteen-year-old who thought nothing of this man she got involved with. No. He had a very normal, (or somewhat normal) enjoyable-to-be-around personality. But as different things occurred, the feelings inside me were going in every direction, and God knew I wasn't able to pull myself out of this mess on my own. God loved me and knew I needed Him to do the work, so He stretched His arms down, plucked me and my helpless child out of the mess we were in, slowly but surely showing us His plans were much better than mine.

CHAPTER 9
But Now What?

You know the saying, 'It's like night and day' or 'From one extreme to the next'? Either one of those is perfect in describing how I felt that next morning compared to mornings before: at peace. Many thanks to God overflowed on that pillow of mine. It sensed somewhat of a new me. Someone who was actually ready to face the life ahead.

You're right to assume I still didn't know what I'd be focusing on. I knew that road was not going to be a smooth, straight, early Sunday morning drive with beautiful things to look at along the way. Nope. But at least it didn't feel like it was going to be a long, windy, pouring-down rain, miserable rush-hour freeway traffic while you're on 'E' experience either.

I savored this refreshing feeling on this first day of the rest of my life. But not only me. This baby. *My* baby. A much better chance that I and, Lord willing, some future husband for me, would both follow the Lord, love one another, and pass much love to our child.

As I got off my bed, got my warm cozy slippers on, and began walking down the stairs, I knew one thing I definitely would see. My mom sitting in front of the fireplace, holding that cigarette, with the biggest smile on her face as I, as usual, would sit on the couch.

I can't remember all we talked about, but I do know peace and joy were just floating around in the air. My mom no longer had to hide anger inside. No more zipping her lip whenever she felt like sharing her opinion about him. She stated over and over again that morning how happy she was and how willing she was to help me adjust to whatever was ahead for me in this new life. My dad also had his grin going ear to ear while giving his morning "So long, Winnipoops. Off to work," quote.

Yes, all those thoughts were wonderful. YIPPIE!! But now what?

I mean, I could only take in that breath of fresh air for a brief time before getting back to reality, wondering what I was to do with my life. No small question. I was far from having a let-go-and-let-God type of thought. I couldn't just sit back and assume a great life would be placed right there on those wrinkly fingers. I knew better. But what? Two quarters at the community college are far from sounding impressive. Not nearly enough time to get much education now, being smack in the middle of my pregnancy. And thinking of living on my own would be like me starting to like coffee. Impossible. But, thankfully, no one was forcing me to do it all right then and there.

First, focus on being healthy and learn what to expect in the next five months. Second, grow closer to God and my church family.

WAIT! CHURCH FAMILY!

My eyes popped open with that thought. *What about that one particular man?*

Mr. Chris Love-At-First-Sight-and-Everything-Went-Into-Slow-Motion-As-Soon-As-I-Saw-Him Petersen. Now sure, I talked ever so briefly with him once, but Greg was right next to me, so, to me, that time didn't count.

Well, how about now? Happily, I felt another new door opening. But was a pregnant, tummy-sticking-out, already a bit overweight, unmarried, no college education, nineteen-year-old, still living with her parents, young woman able to get to know a handsome, single, twenty-two-year-old University of Washington college student, with a decent job, living on his own? How? It just didn't seem possible.

It sure seems like that realization would have me thinking, why even try? Right? Wrong. I didn't feel that way at all. Deep inside I now knew two things. One, after all that happened this last week, anything unexpected can happen, and two, God often does the most fantastic, far-out, and supernatural things.

This time, though, I learned to keep God in front. God, and then my baby. Then, not too far behind the top two, get to know this adorable... um... I mean, this well-educated, young Christian man.

As weeks of Sunday morning and Sunday evening services, along with Wednesday evening prayer meetings, went by, I got to know Chris a bit more. Remember, Emmanuel wasn't a big church. Everyone knew everyone. It's not one of those you go to not noticing who's new and who's not. So if someone new was there, they stood out. And man, he sure stood out to me as each week went by.

The most important thing he shared in one of the first conversations he and I had was what led him to the Lord and what led him to church, both occurring while I was in California. While I was gone, God had begun showing Chris his need for Him. His hunger for understanding the truth then began and, after hearing about this church, he started coming. His testimony sure sounded a lot truer than a certain someone else's testimony, that's for sure. I also found out he had another year at the university before getting his degree as a landscape architect. Somehow it got brought up that he wasn't looking to start any relationship and was concentrating on studying the Bible, plus his classes at the UW. That was good, I had to tell myself, because I knew I, too, needed to concentrate on my own growth and knowledge of Christ. That, plus focusing on having my child in about four months.

As the next month or two went by, it was getting easier for me being pregnant, both physically and emotionally. For quite a few months after our pastor's wife had her baby, I was the only one pregnant at church. Fortunately, it wasn't too long before other ladies had gotten pregnant. I admit, I felt a little wiser than normal in passing along pregnancy information I had learned. They were all married, but I didn't feel one speck of discomfort talking with them about the pros and cons of being pregnant. I know there were many nights my pillow could tell I was filled with joy, knowing I could share my experience of God holding me through it all with my dear friends at church. I must say, I liked conversations with a few of those ladies, especially when those conversations would turn into sentences like, "Marianne, how about we go talk over there, closer to where Chris is."

Yep. As time went by, everyone could see that he and I got along great, and since Chris and I were pretty much the only single adults, it's no wonder more than just me was thinking that. *I love what others are thinking and that it's not just me.*

I didn't know if Chris was aware of any of this. I never really asked, "Hey, Chris. Do you think, along with me and everyone else here, that we should be an item?"

We just talked about this-and-that's, Pastor Mark's messages, Chris's classes, life at the basement he was renting close to the university, my tummy discomforts, my new job watching kids at the YMCA daycare, his dog he had growing up, my dog growing up, me playing saxophone, him playing drums, and other things we had in common. What I didn't share with him, however, was how I made sure I polished my fingernails right before each Wednesday night prayer meeting.

I was so thankful that my church was a true family of believers. Great messages, great fellowship. As my tummy was slowly but surely getting bigger, my love for all I was learning was growing as well. My church family helped me hang on with my family situation at home.   Friction that had been going on for years between my parents was growing. Thankfully, I knew my soap-opera life wasn't making it worse. I actually think it might have been helping, as it got them thinking of other things instead of what was wrong between them.

My siblings' lives, too, were all going in different directions.

It seemed they were all hoping they could find greener grass elsewhere. Christ wasn't included on their road in life. It was good that I could escape not only on Sundays, but at the Wednesday evening prayer meetings too. Sort of a mid-week refreshment. It's scary to think how less peaceful I would have felt during that time if I didn't have a great source for spiritual support and friends.

A part-time job I got at the YMCA was enjoyable and filled up some of my empty hours. Looking after little kindergarten-aged children did a few things for me. It helped me pass the time; helped me make a little money; and helped me realize I'm going to have a child this age really soon.

Kind of weird thinking the third one, that's for sure. But I didn't mind, for I was learning important things. Being the youngest of seven, I had never really been around younger kids on a daily basis. Sure, I did have a little time with Kelly's two boys around, two years and four years old. But that didn't count. I knew they were cute, crazy little boys, and I had fun being an aunt once every few weeks for a few hours. But seeing different kids at this daycare every day was profitable for me, realizing how parents play a big role in their child's life.

I sensed something in one little boy, that his home life wasn't that positive, and I can, to this day, still picture how his face was either sad or mad, with words to match his look. He caused me to think how I wanted my own baby to grow up instead, with sweet smiles to pass around.

If you remember, I wrote early on that as a teen I was not—oh, how should I word it—'slender.' I wasn't obese or fat, but just a little too chubby and embarrassed to wear any type of dress. Especially how I looked wearing my senior-year prom dress. Well-rounded describes it perfectly. Being pregnant now didn't help. I mostly wore big sweatshirts. So during this pregnancy, I, Marianne Baggy-Sweatshirt Houstoun, was even more embarrassed.

"Oh, Marianne, you just look pregnant," many would say. My doctor gave me no cause to worry about my weight either.

"You're growing the normal amount. As a matter of fact, you might be a little less than normal." Have I said yet I loved my doctor? She was a godsend, seriously. Suggested by our family doctor, she was a dear woman, looking to be in her early thirties. Something she said that first time I saw her caused us to share that we were both Christians, thus creating a few great conversations as the months went by. She became such an encouragement to me. Like I said, a godsend.

No one really knew how I felt inside. No, not what the baby felt like inside, but how my heart felt inside from being a bit overweight *and* pregnant. I tried to hide the fact I was pregnant for as long as I could. And, actually, being a bit overweight helped. As another month or so went by, I still preferred to look a little overweight instead of a little pregnant. When I got to be about four or five months along, I became more at peace with it all and just gave in, content to show the world I was with child. I was actually relieved when I couldn't hide it any longer. That is, until I was reading about weight *after* the baby is born. Boy, was I scared.

Oh, great. I'm already big and will most likely gain MORE! UGH!

But by this point I wasn't the only one pregnant. Having others at church expecting really helped. Don't get me wrong. It's not like seeing others pregnant had me smiling ear to ear every morning— my mirror kept me from doing that, but I no longer felt alone in this.

Even with everything going on inside, God was obviously there, holding me and keeping me from feeling too down and out. Actually, my entire pregnancy was rather easy. Remember that one time I threw up? That was still the only time. True, day in and day out I worried about my weight, but aside from that, most things seemed good. An easy pregnancy and not being stressed at my daycare job were sure nice. Aside from that friction between my parents, it was all pretty low key, with no real pressure at home. Heck, I even had my own car I had gotten my senior year.

One sweet Capri it was. So it wasn't too long before I started to love thinking how this baby I was feeling moving around inside was going to be just mine. Well, mine and God's.

Hmmm. What should I call her?

Being that I had free time, I often watched TV. I'll never forget watching a certain soap opera then. (Yes, one bad side effect from having tons of free time many afternoons in a row, soap operas.) One in particular was my favorite. While watching it one day, one of the character's names really stood out, one I hadn't noticed before. Cassie. No, not Cassandra. Just Cassie.

THAT'S IT! Cassie! Cassie Houstoun. I like that a lot. PERFECT! But what for a middle name? Hmmm.

Now to explain why I knew to think of a girl's name. I was one who had heard about the good old Drano test. Nowadays you can go to Google and see what that is, but back then you listened to your friends tell you about it.

"Cool! Sounds like a test I can do! Here, let me write it down to make sure I do it right. I'll let you know Sunday what it says."

So there I was in the bathroom, eager to do the Drano test. I think I read the directions ninety-nine times, thinking the more I read it, the better chance the results would show a girl. *Let's see here. If the color changes to a dark color, it's a boy. If it's a greenish color or has not changed, it's a girl. Oh, my gosh. I sure hope I did the mixing right.*

Right then I couldn't help but feel how this was similar to six months prior when I was staring at a bit of pee in a cup. This time I felt a lot more at peace, but still nervous.

Is it... is it changing? It looks like it's... IT'S A GIRL!

You should have seen my face when that color stayed put. No change.

A GIRL! A GIRL! A GIRL!

Sure, I knew it wasn't an official test, knowing doctors wouldn't swear by it, but it sure helped me look forward to seeing what this wiggly thing inside me was going to be. Don't worry. I knew if it was going to be a boy, I'd still be thrilled to pieces about it. I guess thinking pink was a different type of thrill. A mommy-and-daughter thrill.

I loved that Drano test.

CHAPTER 10
Man, I'm Daring

Let's see. Where are we?

– I got pregnant.

– Almost got married.

– That unforgettable goodbye to Greg.

– Those unforgettable hellos to Chris at church.

– Working at the YMCA daycare.

– Cherishing my family at church.

– Pregnancy, thus far, very easy.

– Cassie for her name.

Now I'm sure I'd be so much more drained if I had a full-time job, was going to school, had more kids, had to think of making grocery lists plus do all the shopping, or lived in a house that needed tons of work done. But for me at this point, I had more extra time than perhaps many in my situation. Believe me, I'm not complaining. I did offer my time to help Mom, driving here or there to get this or that. I offered to help Dad by grabbing the newspaper from outside the front door, but for sure never mowed that lawn. My job at the daycare helped fill some time, but that was pretty much it.

So with that free time, I thought of that certain man I was slowly getting to know. Chris Petersen. By this point he was well aware of all I went through, my time in California, the reasons why the wedding was canceled, and what life was like living with my parents. He was kind, friendly, and sincere whenever we talked, which kept proving even more that love at first sight can be real.

After a few months had passed, conversations were becoming pretty routine as people gathered to gab. Church was the only place we were able to talk, since he lived about thirty minutes away, renting someone's basement close to the University of Washington. That location made it impossible for me to 'accidentally' run into him at a store. But one day he told a few of us at church how he had just started staying at someone's home from church for a month or so, watching their few farm animals while they were out of town. Get this. That house was only five minutes from church. Better yet, five minutes from my house.

I have to figure out some way to stop by. Hmmm, I know! Well, it's ALMOST just he and I, anyway.

"Chris, a few days next week I'll be babysitting my two nephews. Those two I've told you about, John and Danny, five and two years old. Days can get pretty boring for them, so I thought, since you're watching those animals, I know they would love to see them. It would help me, too, to fill up some of that time." What a good idea! I mean, I *am* telling the truth.

"That sounds like a neat idea," Chris responded. "I don't see why not."

"Oh, good," I said as we then discussed the best day and time. *It worked! It worked! I can't believe it. It WORKED!*

"Thanks, Chris. Friday should be perfect. They'll love it." (Yes, you have my permission to replace the 'They'll' with 'I'll.')

A few days later, "Okay, guys, time to see some cool animals. Ready?" *I know I sure am.*

They were so excited. They couldn't wait to get there. *Look relaxed, Marianne. Yes, you're six months pregnant, but forget that and just look relaxed.*

I can still picture Chris walking out on the driveway to meet us. *Stop staring, Marianne. Stop staring.*

"Hi, Chris. This is John and Danny. John and Danny, say hi," as they stepped out of the car, staying close to me.

"Hi," they said in unison.

"Thanks so much for letting us come over to see the animals. The boys couldn't wait."

"You're welcome. Here, guys, follow me."

That was the start to the best ninety minutes I'd had in forever. Okay, maybe not forever, but almost. Chris and I walked around the two-acre fenced-in yard as the boys got up close to a few different animals. Not many, just a few. Two or so cows, some chickens, a few ducks, with one or two others. I wasn't really paying that much attention to them, and I'm sure you know why. What I noticed most is that Chris and I talked a little bit differently. Not being in the normal church-ish atmosphere was why. More personal. Naturally there was some conversation about those animals and what it was like housesitting, and there was talk about my two nephews and life as an aunt. But more than that. It's not like there were any deep discussions about any huge subjects. It was all a bit light, but, well, different. A positive difference.

Oh, this is nice. Just he and I, talking. No other adults around. I could get used to this.

My thoughts continued on as ten minutes passed, twenty minutes passed, sixty minutes passed.

Sad to say, all the animals had been seen. I won't say finally, because finally makes it sound like you *want* time to come to an end. I sure didn't. But I couldn't make it too obvious how I had planned this with ulterior motives. When both boys began showing the I'm-bored look, I forced myself to say we should get going.

Walking to the car I, of course, had to tell the boys, "Say thank you."

"Thank you," both said, while avoiding looking directly at Chris.

"You're welcome, John and Danny," he replied.

"Thanks for letting the boys come by. It made this day so much more fun for them. See you on Sunday." I wanted to add one more sentence, "And thanks for being so handsome to gaze at while listening to your beautiful tone of voice. Goodbye."

Off we drove. I was overflowing with wonder. *What's he thinking? What's he thinking? I know what I'm thinking. I wish he had to watch those animals for an entire year. I wonder what he's thinking. I love babysitting.*

A few days later was Sunday and, I must say, it felt just a hair different than the Sunday before. From a distance we met eye to eye. Just a tiny, different look between us. Not the normal look you give to everyday acquaintances. Nope. More of that look you give after you've, well, shared an hour talking, with animals all around. Hard to explain, but it sort of gave an official feel, like we could do a bit more talking, just the two of us.

From then on our talking did occur a bit more frequently. More telling about our pasts, goals for our futures, along with spiritual topics. As more weeks went by, Sunday mornings, Sunday evenings, and Wednesday evenings, it got to be pretty normal that we'd both be some of the last ones there talking. I wasn't the only one thinking this, but other people began to notice. I do have to state, however, that nothing definite had started, but I do give credit for this sweet change to that one day babysitting. Glad I was daring.

My visits to the doctor remained all nice and normal. By now I was about seven months along and still going smoothly. All my maternity clothes were pretty much from thrift stores and, man, was I glad it wasn't much longer I'd be wearing them. These last few months, however, the doctor did tell me totally unexpected news.

A bit overweight, big sweatshirts were my normal attire. And we all know the weight gained during pregnancy isn't such an enjoyable fact to accept. But out of the blue, after I got my routine weight checked, she said, "No real worry, but I must say you are not the weight you should be by now."

"Oh, great. I need to watch my weight? I'm gaining too much?" I asked.

"No. Actually, you haven't gained the amount of weight that is normal. You need to eat a bit more for that baby. Are you dieting at all?" she asked.

"No. I'm not eating tons of junk, but not dieting."

"Well, just eat more good food. More than you have been," she instructed. "From now on, each time you come in, I want to see a few more pounds than the normal gain you should be showing. Understand?"

Understand? With the biggest grin, I understood. On the way to each doctor's visit from then on, I stopped and grabbed a good old foot-long sandwich across the street from the doctor's office. After all, I had to make sure I would show the most weight gain possible, right? Since I currently live in the same area, I still giggle inside every time I drive past that Subway.

Feeling this baby inside was getting more uncomfortable. Not too bad, though. Deciding if I would nurse or bottle feed was my main dilemma. No nursing mom really to follow, since there was only one baby before mine at church. My sister, who had John and Danny, didn't live there when her boys were babies, so I didn't have anyone around that I could witness nursing. And remember, no YouTube back then to see how it's done.

My doctor strongly encouraged me to, and I gulped down every little bit of information, agreeing it was better to nurse. Was I brave enough to try nursing this new human being I was soon to have? Would I dare to feel the discomfort I was warned about? Would I dare to let people watch me nurse? How about getting used to nursing bras, nursing pads, and looking even larger than I started out? Was I daring enough to have spur-of-the-moment milk leaks that I was told would happen? Yes, I was daring enough. I kept telling myself that I should. I felt I had to at least try to do what I felt was best. *I can do it. I can do it.*

I planned to work a bit longer at the daycare. I was very thankful for that job, but I wasn't going to miss it too much. I began to enjoy picturing myself caring for my very own little baby.

I kinda liked that thought more instead of telling little four – and five-year-olds to share their toys.

Journal Time. Yep, it's time to share more of my journal and what was going from my heart to the paper at this time in my pregnancy. I wish I hadn't allowed there to be a huge gap between writings. You need to know that... oh, my journal will tell you. See if you can notice a few things I leave out.

Jan 2, 1987

How to even begin to explain the past year and a half? The best way to start is with the numero-uno step in my life, and that is being Born Again in Christ Jesus. Yes, I'm a new creature and will be rocking for Jesus for all eternity. September 10 of 1985 is when it happened. Now Eyde is no longer 'religious'! She, Willma, and I are all sisters in Christ! Jesus is my life now, and not the things of this world.

Okay, let's see. A lot has happened. April of '86 I drove down to Santa Maria and lived with Debbie for three months, worked at the Hilton Hotel in room service. On my return home I was faced with my niece's tumor and seeing her die. She died in September. So sad. In the meantime, God showed me the direction my life was to take. He gave me a baby. As of this writing, I am seven-and-a-half months along in my pregnancy. Things are fine as long as Jesus is close by. If it wasn't for His will for my life, I'd go crazy! I'm making it through just fine. Praise God!

Trouble on the home front. Mom and Dad aren't getting along. If they aren't separated soon, then I'll be surprised. Oh, Jesus, please save them. Save all my family. Kelly's husband is out of the Army and they are also living here at Mom and Dad's until they get settled. Oh, and the space shuttle blew up since I last wrote. It's been a very tough year.

I'm sort of surprised I didn't write for almost two years. *What?* Quick update: I started my journal when I was twelve. Every day for a while, then every other day, then every other week, then every other month, then maybe half a year and, at this point, a few years' break. You mean I didn't write at all during this entire time? I know, I know, crazy. I still ponder why I didn't write at all about when I moved to California, met Greg, came back home, found out I was pregnant, almost got married, said good riddance to the one I almost married, was thrilled with the Drano test, and started to get to know this one gorgeous man from church. How I wish I had. I would love to have read not so much about how terribly guilty I felt, but much more about how obvious it was to me that God carried me through it all. I guess I was going through so much turmoil, I didn't want to remember it by putting it on paper. I'm just glad I got back into writing.

CHAPTER 11
No Longer Me, Myself, and I

You've heard the old saying 'Never go to an energetic concert a few nights before your due date,' right? Okay, I made that up, but I can't help but give advice to you all. Don't go to an energetic concert a few nights before your due date. Even if it's a Christian concert. If my pillow could scream, I'm sure it would have told me what a crazy idea that was. After all, my pillow also had terrible nights those last few weeks, just as I had. Me rolling around, trying to find some comfortable position in bed, I'm sure made the pillow dread bedtime and want to scream "BE STILL, MARIANNE!" By this time I was so uncomfortable, rolling back and forth, back and forth. Extra pillows between my knees, between my feet, blankets on, blankets off, legs straight, legs bent.

Please, baby. Come out NOW! Even my thoughts in the afternoons weren't so great. *Oh, good, in about nine hours I can go through all that again.*

A nice interruption one night, however. Yep, going to a concert. Something much better to think about all day instead of 'It's almost time to go to bed.'

"Bye, Mom. Don't worry. Willma and I will be very careful wherever we park. Baby and I are fine. Bye."

In a few days my life would change majorly, so this concert was a perfect distraction. What a great time, just hanging out with Willma, surrounded by tons of other people, listening to music we loved, knowing every word of every song.

I sure noticed people looking at me, most likely thinking I was a bit crazy being there with my stomach sticking 'out to here,' but oh well, I didn't mind. After all, I felt great. We had a ball just singing right along with people crammed all around us. One of those concerts where everyone stood up the entire time, swaying back and forth.

Concert done. Willma and I totally enjoyed it. Darn it, back to real life. That was one night I'm sure Willma loved living just two houses down, because it was so late when I got dropped off. Certainly one of the best parts about going was how thinking about it in bed afterward distracted me from my pain. WOOHOO!

What also helped was knowing the next day was a birthday party for someone from church: Ralph, the one who had first told me about Emmanuel. He was married by then, so he and his wife planned a little birthday shebang at their place with friends from church. I knew Chris would be there, so of course I was thinking lots about that. *And this is really the first time for a friendly gathering outside of church since I started going there. If I'm there and he's there... I'd better make sure I do my nails tomorrow.* Nice thoughts, indeed, on that pillow.

But, I must say, it wasn't all happy-go-lucky thinking for very long that night. No. My pillow could sense a more calm, serious mind in there as well.

I'm probably gonna have this baby any day now. Tonight was probably the last time of having fun with Willma for a long time. And tomorrow will be my last time doing things with friends from church for a while as well.

My pillow sensed lots of up-and-down, up-and down thoughts. Fun time at the concert on my mind, yes. Me, myself, and I time, so nice to have, yes. But thoughts, too, of how my life would be changing very soon. The newness of having a baby in my arms soon filled my mind. I already thought a lot about all this, mind you, but that night I just pleaded with God a bit more to hold me through all the changes. From 'me' time to 'mom' time. Give tons of care to my very own little baby and give less to myself. Any day now.

Now don't feel sad for me at all. I contemplated good thoughts on that night too. That time away from the world, lying down on my pillow, was golden. My pillow was more perfect that night than most nights. It was one of the reasons I finally fell asleep. Most likely, I fell asleep thinking of, you guessed it, seeing Chris the next evening.

Zzzzz

6:30 a.m. that next day

Oh, this uncomfortable baby. Why, oh why does it have to feel like this? Come on, baby. Relax and let me sleep.

I can picture it now, as if I were a bug on the wall looking down at myself lying flat on my back.

I know I feel uncomfortable in bed now all the time, but... but what's this weird feeling? This isn't normal, is it? No. NO!

Just then, yep, MY WATER BROKE! EEK! Twenty-million thoughts began.

Water breaking. Great. Now what? Where's Mom? I have to call Kelly. Where's my stuff I packed? This is gross. Ick. When do I start breathing weird? I'M ABOUT TO BECOME A MOM! I need to find Mom. Wait, I'd better clean a bit of this up first.

When done, I calmly and quietly walked downstairs. Why calm? Because as I began walking down, I heard my dad in the kitchen eating his routine bowl of cereal with fruit. I just wasn't ready to face Dad and say "Good morning, Dad. That cereal looks good. By the way, my water broke."

No, I wasn't ready for his response that early in the morning. Fortunately I knew he'd be going to work very soon. I tried my best at hiding the increasing amount of pain I was feeling.

"Dad, where's Mom?" I nonchalantly asked, not having seen her by the fireplace.

"I bet she'll be down soon. I think I heard her moving around up there," he said while finishing his last spoonful of cereal.

"Bye, Dad," I finally got to say, thankfully, only a few minutes later.

"Bye, Winnipoops."

Garage door opens. Car goes out. Garage door closes.

"MOM! MY WATER BROKE!"

She was on her way down the stairs, probably thinking she'd sit by the fireplace and try to prep for the new day, when she heard that.

"REALLY? OH, MY WORD," as she stared at my tummy. "Are you all right?"

While sitting on a chair in the kitchen, holding my tummy, I explained how it all happened. More pain. Glad I didn't have to hide it anymore. *Really* glad. I stayed on that chair as we counted how many minutes between contractions. Mom called Kelly.

"Hi, Kelly. I know it's early, but only because it's time! She's fine. I'll call again when it gets to be five minutes between contractions." It was planned that Kelly would be my supporter, being she'd had two kids as of late and I cherished all the support she had given me through this entire pregnancy. She, for sure, was the one.

It wasn't very long, perhaps thirty minutes or so, before it got to that five-minute point. (Felt like thirty hours.) Off we went. I don't believe I have ever seen Mom drive so fast. So there I was, at the hospital, face-to-face with reality. I, Marianne Almost-A-Mom Houstoun, was going to have my very own baby.

But when? I had assumed my story would be like so many others I heard or read: twelve, sixteen, twenty hours of labor, perhaps. Thanks, but no thanks. But there was nothing I could do about it. I had already told myself that if the pain got too hard, I would gladly have an epidural.

Different workers at the hospital were all around me, checking all those this-and-that's. Finally my doctor showed up totally relaxed, as if delivering a baby was like making a peanut butter and jelly sandwich. I'm sure God heard me requesting, twenty-million times, "Oh, God, please help me!" as the contractions got closer. An hour went by. Contractions got closer. More pain. Kelly holding my hand, saying, "Relax. You can do it."

Breeeeathe... breeeeathe... MAN, I DON'T LIKE THIS! Breeeeathe... breeeeathe.

Tons of hours to go, I assumed. Tick-tock, tick-tock. It was five hours since my water broke. Felt like fifty. I knew then what 'eternity' meant. I eventually had to ask, in sort of a joking manner, "I'm too young to go through all this pain. Could I have my epidural now? Please?"

I will never forget my doctor's answer. "It's too late. The baby's coming out right now. Time to push."

WHAT? NOT EVEN SIX HOURS? (Push. Puuuush.) *Seriously! NOW? She's GOT to be... OOWWWWW!*

Time for that one-two-three breathing to start while closing my eyes really tight and hearing my sister say, calmly but firmly, "Puuuuuuuuuush."

The thoughts of, *I wonder what this baby will look like, I hope I'll be a good mom, I hope it sleeps well at night,* were NOT the ones going through my head. Instead, *Man, this hurts! I can't do this! When will this be over?*

That hour of pushing was the slowest hour ever but also the fastest. Then it got to the point where, any second now, I was about to be a mom.

"Here she comes. Here she comes. Puuuuuuuush. Here she... is."

The next thing I saw answered the question only my pillow and I knew about: how I'd feel the first time I'd see my baby. That baby I'm seeing is her. That baby girl I'm seeing is mine. My baby, I instantly love her. What just happened? I was amazed at this bundle being handed to me. Every other thought, every other worry, every concern, every question, faded away. This life, this adorable real doll, was now all wrapped up and placed in my very own arms.

The I'm-a-mom thought wasn't there. Instead, *She's my own precious baby. Cassie. Cassie Angelyn Houstoun. My daughter. She's mine. God, thank You.*

Total peace. On top of that, I was completely awake and full of energy! This quick labor and delivery right after a fairly normal night's sleep left me overflowing with thanks to God. I was so THERE! Completely energized, wanting to just gaze at that beautiful little gift. That gift that felt so mine.

Time to share my new gift with others. Kelly, who, of course, was already there. My mom, after coming in, couldn't wait to hold Cassie. I loved looking at my mom. She was sure one happy-looking grandma. But then all the weighing, measuring, instructions on what to expect, also were taking place. That much-needed step-by-step guidance on how to nurse finally began. Time was given to cover all that necessary baby info with people all around. And then Willma arrived. She and I joked on how all the standing and swaying back and forth during the concert must have caused this to happen today.

But then the time came for Cassie and me to be alone in that hospital room.

I... am now... a mom. That kept running through my head until more practical thoughts gradually started to form. *I hope I'm holding her right.* Before I knew it, thoughts began overflowing. *What if I accidentally drop her? What if I don't have good-enough milk? What about sleeping? What about changing diapers? Money! What about paying for more diapers? WASHING those diapers! What will sleeping be like?* And on and on and on. The thought arose, too, of how I needed to write a letter to Greg and his parents about the birth of this baby.

But in the midst of all those thoughts, God guided my eyes to see a small box of microscopic Band-aids on the little table next to me. I had to take one out to gaze at the tininess of it. *These are so PUNY!* I couldn't help but smile and get back to simply thanking God for this perfect daughter I now had in my arms. Cassie Angelyn Houstoun.

It wasn't that long before nurses came in again to check things out while getting everything set for me to spend the night. Early evening had arrived when something dawned on me. Something I hadn't given one thought to all day. (Golly, I wonder why?) That thought? Chris Petersen.

I won't get to see Chris tonight. If I'm not there, then he won't think of me. Selfish, I know. I had the best reason in the world why I couldn't make it, but still... An important question formed. *How can I get him to at least think of me for one split second?* Hmmm. A few minutes of pondering. *I know what will work!*

I looked in my purse, got my phone list out, and grabbed that room's telephone. Ring, ring. Ring, ring.

Ralph answered, "Hello," as I could hear gabbing in the background.

"Hi, Ralph. This is Marianne," I tried to say as nonchalantly as possible. Didn't want to have the I-just-became-a-mom tone of voice. "Happy birthday, Ralph! I'm just calling to explain why I'm not able to come to your party tonight. Nothing big, just... well, I just had my baby today."

"MARIANNE HAD HER BABY TODAY!" he hollered so everyone at his place could hear. Tons of cheering suddenly erupted. 'YAY' and 'CONGRATULATIONS' could be heard from far off. I then shared a few simple facts like time, size, weight, the normal things all new moms share. Shortly after, the goodbyes were passed back and forth. Click.

There. Chris just thought about me. Mission accomplished.

CHAPTER 12
First Times

Going up that driveway with Mom driving wasn't weird. We'd done that oodles and oodles of times. What was weird was it being the first time going up that driveway with me as a mom! My first time ever in a car with my very own daughter, all cozy in her car seat. First time ever on that dead-end, going up that driveway, about to go into her very first home. Pulling that car seat out for the first time as it held my precious baby daughter. I'll never forget how that felt.

"Here, let me grab all the stuff," Mom offered.

I saw Kelly's car. *OH, GOODY. John and Danny can see her now.* Dad, however, was still at work, as it was a Tuesday afternoon.

I came up to the door thinking how my life in that house as a mom had officially begun. I knew Cassie, this delicate sleeping treasure, would make everyone inside that house melt and say 'AHH.' John and Danny would probably have their eyes wide open, tiptoeing over, whispering, "Is that the baby?"

I opened the door and took a few steps in, quietly saying, "We're here," slowly walking down the hallway to the kitchen. "Anyone want to see their cute little cousin?" I asked. Suddenly I heard the loudest five-year-old in the world, waving a long stick (oh, excuse me, I mean a long sword) all around while jumping as he ran straight toward Cassie, "Hiiii-ya! Let me show her what I can do with my sword!" he screeched. Not quite what I expected.

"NO, JOHN! Not at the baby!" Kelly hollered while my arms

snuggled around Cassie, quickly scooting away from him. No harm done. Just a memory there is no way I can forget.

"Oh, she's so cute!" were the only words said that next hour. Mom made sure I knew she would do anything, at the drop of a hat, for me or Cassie.

My dad sure smiled when he got home. A true granddad's face. And David? A true uncle's face right there as well.

I wonder what it's going to be like from now on, knowing I'm this baby's mom?

After a few short hours had passed, I experienced my first time saying, "I gotta go upstairs now and feed the baby." I wasn't at all used to this new mommy thing, and I wasn't ready yet to say 'nurse.' It sounded too official for something I wasn't ready for. The best way to say it would have been, "I gotta go upstairs now and be totally uncomfortable and unsure of what the heck I'm doing."

But I was committed to nurse. I knew it was best, even if I really wasn't looking forward to it. I had no excuse not to, so I encouraged myself by thinking anything is easy now if you've experienced giving birth. Also, the nurses at the hospital made it sound like my efforts there went great and all should go fine.

Once home, though, new thoughts arose about nursing. I decided I didn't want anyone at home to watch me. I felt it best to just do it in my room, I mean, *OUR* room. Something about having a baby sucking on my breast while I was on the couch in the living room didn't really appeal to me, even if I was covered with a blanket. I wasn't ready to have my brother David walk in as I was nursing Cassie while watching something on the TV. No, thanks. Sorry. Or how about Dad walking by holding the newspaper as I'm at the kitchen table nursing? I don't think so. Neither of these for a while, anyway.

This is gonna be OUR place, Cassie. Our hiding place for feeding.

It wasn't easy. I knew from all the facts I had been told that the first couple days wouldn't be peachy-keen. So as those first few tries went by, I just kept smiling. No worries. It was uncomfortable getting her all adjusted on me correctly, but I got used to it more as each attempt went by.

Time now for our first night, March 10, in my... wait, I have to get used to calling it OUR room, as a family, as mommy and daughter. After wondering for nine months what it would be like, our first night at home had finally arrived. My last attempt nursing that first full day—or at least trying to nurse—now done. Tired? Not too bad, but time on my pillow was needed far more than going back downstairs. Me, lights out, thinking about this new life with my new daughter now in the crib next to my bed. Marianne Mom Houstoun and Cassie's very first time going to bed in THEIR room.

First time my pillow heard me thanking God for so much. A very short and easy time in labor, for sure, but mainly that Cassie seemed to be a true piece of gold. My thoughts were filled with joy, wonder, worry, thrill, but still a bit scared.

I'm sure if that night in 1987 was now 2018, I would have taken a selfie of me holding my adorable daughter. But more so I'd have gotten in bed, grabbed my laptop, opened up Google, and typed in 'Peace as a new mom' or 'Parenting skills' or, better yet, 'How is a nineteen-year-old supposed to be a good mom?' But no. No laptops or iPhones then. Only my pillow, darkness, and my thoughts. I knew many little this-and-that's from reading I had done, plus info others had shared with me at home or at church. But that night all I could do was think and pray. *Thank you so much, Lord, for Cassie. But please help me know what I'm doing.*

That then started me thanking Him for the easy pregnancy, no real morning sickness, my caring family, a decent job, encouraging, dear friends at church, to Him even giving me a Christian doctor. I'm sure I even smiled on my pillow, glad I had the okay to pig out at Subway on the way to that doctor. So many things God did for me those nine months. And, to top it off, having it end with that incredibly short, six-hour delivery. He had obviously shown me He was still holding me.

I don't remember what my last thoughts were that first night as a mom, but at last, with God's help, I managed to fall asleep. Not for long, though. I woke up a bit disoriented after hearing some sound I'd never heard before. I think even my pillow was confused.

Wha... what's tha... what's that sound? Oh! THAT sound! Cassie! Oh, great. I need to feed her.

My hungry daughter. The night before in the hospital had been totally different than this one at home. This new sound was foreign. They spoiled me at the hospital, making sure I could rest, so I didn't get a real taste of what it would be like to be awakened for feedings. That night I knew.

I'm sure not used to this type of thinking in the middle of the night.

Something good did come out of this midnight attempt to nurse. I learned how wonderful it is to just nurse in bed! Then, after giving it my best, to just lie down with Cassie next to me. After making sure I was following all the rules on how to hold her correctly, I loved being cozy with my infant on my bed at night. I'm sure my pillow had its thoughts on all this newness going on as well. It had to adjust to me moving it around a bit so I could get comfortable, correctly holding the newest member of the family.

Now, if you can recall, most mornings I'd come downstairs, still in my pj's, and sit on the couch in the living room while my mom was smoking in front of the empty fireplace. This next morning was sort of the same, the difference being that today I walked down holding my daughter. As we came into the room, my mom's smile went from ear to ear, forgetting for a while all the other things she was thinking about.

Of course she asked, "So how did she sleep? How did you sleep?" I'm sure I told her all about it without too much complaining.

"I just hope she lets me sleep better soon."

All day was fairly easy, just sitting around holding my baby. There was really only one thing I didn't find true joy in. Nursing! Not comfortable at all. But I was determined.

God will help me. She won't die yet. I can do it. I have to. Keep trying, Marianne. Keep trying. I continued to go into our room to nurse. The thought of bottles would pop up. *NO, MARIANNE! Bottles are NOT right. Stop thinking that!*

Another day went by. Cassie was getting a little milk, but still, I could tell it wasn't enough. And it sure wasn't comfortable on my end of it all either. No one was around for me to ask for any nursing secrets. My mom was there, yes, but she had never nursed any of us kids, so not much advice from her. Websites, where were you back then?

Toward the end of that second or third day being home, I was still trying to make that perfect picture of me nursing, completely relaxed, full of joy, gazing at Cassie's face. No go. Far from it.

I'll never forget one hour. I can still picture myself on that chair in my room, door shut. I think I can even recall what clothes I had on. One small tear started to form. *Oh, this... this is just not... not what I thought.*

Before I knew it, a downpour of tears began.

I can't. I can't! I CANNOT do this anymore! I just can't! What about those few things I read that said formula isn't really that bad? They're just not as good for the baby as breast milk, but it's not bad for the baby. The thought of bottle feeding began to grow.

Kelly used formula with John and Danny and they're fine.

Am I sounding convincing yet?

I'm a single mom, and it would really be helpful if others could feed Cassie. I don't have a husband to help.

Can you tell yet what I was convincing myself to do? Here's a final clue:

And if I did, I could go places with her really soon, like to church! And then I could see Chris!

Decision made.

Formula, here I come. Cassie won't die. I'll be happy, which means Cassie will have a better mom!

A huge grin on my face now.

I won't be locked in my room anymore, bawling my head off!

Talk about one humbling experience. Me, admitting I couldn't be a mom on my own; I needed help. After thinking about all this, peace of mind showed up when deciding a bottle would be perfect for my daughter. Heck, it began to sound so great that I even wanted one for myself.

"Mom," I humbly said, looking around for her as I came down holding Cassie. (Of course I changed my shirt before coming down, to hide the proof I had bawled my head off.) "Mom, I just came to the conclusion that I'm going to give her formula. Nursing isn't working out. Could you hold her for a few minutes while I run out and get some?"

"Marianne, I couldn't help but think how you might change your mind," she said while giving me a warm grin. "I just so happen to have gotten a little batch of it for you, just in case. I'll go get it."

Right then and there I decided I loved my mom even more. There were still a few bottles in the cupboard from when Danny needed them, so it wasn't long before another first: first time making an unforgettable bottle of formula for Cassie, worth, to me, a million dollars.

I must have read the directions forty-eight—no—forty-nine times, making sure the right amount of formula and water were mixed the right way. Getting it to the best temperature was my next mission. Anything was better than trying to nurse. That first time holding Cassie, giving her that bottle, watching her have her first real meal while her face showed that died-and-gone-to-heaven look. It was obvious she loved it. Marianne Loves-Bottles Houstoun also looked at *her* mom, the best grandma in the world.

Yes, I probably did have a little discomfort from all of a sudden not nursing, but I think since I never really had made a normal amount of milk by then, it wasn't that bad. Either that or I was just so happy, I didn't even notice.

All these different first times. The next major first time was one

I had a hard time waiting for. Going to church for the, you got it, first time as a mom. Knowing my baby was getting enough food, finally, I felt ready to actually show her off. At church, Pastor Mark and his wife were the only ones with a baby at that point, so when we showed up (I have to get used to saying 'we'), many were saying 'oooh' and 'ahhh' while staring. I loved it. I looked at each person's eyes as I showed her off, seeing what I hoped for, those melting facial expressions. All the ladies needed their turn holding Cassie while asking me for more details about the delivery. By this time, those few other women in the congregation who were now pregnant wanted me to share a little info on what to expect.

It felt so nice feeling fellow believers' encouragement and support for me. But I will admit, what really stood out was seeing Chris coming over. The first time Chris sees me holding my very own daughter. I did have a few worried thoughts.

Maybe he sees me holding this baby, which then makes him far from liking a nineteen-year-old single mom. He gets closer. *Don't melt, Marianne, don't melt. You're holding your baby.*

Now remember, we weren't boyfriend and girlfriend; we were just friends. I don't remember what he first said when he saw Cassie. It was probably the typical, "Oh, how cute," but to me it was *who* said it and not so much what was said. I just knew that me being a mother now didn't change one speck of how I felt about him. But what I wondered, for the first time then and there, was if him seeing me holding this baby, seeing me as an official mom, could sort of scare him off. On second thought, maybe that's good! Maybe Marianne with an adorable baby is better than Marianne who's pregnant. I sort of liked that second thought.

Okay, now what? A lot to be thankful for, but now what? I just had a baby. Delivery went great. Peace now, after days trying to nurse. My new name: Marianne Loves-Bottles Houstoun. A master at getting bottles ready for the nighttime feedings. A pro at changing diapers. And now, taking Cassie to church, getting into a normal routine.

Yep, things were looking good. After a few more weeks went by, I was thrilled at my weight! Remember how I hadn't gained enough weight those last few months? Well, it turns out that all the weight I did gain came off easily, *and more!* I don't know why in the world that happened, but I sure wasn't complaining. Too bad I couldn't sell this secret diet and make millions. I was so uncomfortable with my weight before, so I added this to my list of God's many blessings. He spoiled me by even having me weigh less than before I got pregnant. He, alone, I give credit to. Nothing I did, that's for sure.

But, like I have said before, now what? Me. Cassie. The bottles. Day in and day out. Now what? I sure didn't know. All the little routines of life as a mom were going fine. More often than not I went downstairs to relax on my friend, the couch, talking to you-know-who in front of that you-know-what, chatting about how sleeping at night was going or where I could find the best formula for a good price, or if I could watch John and Danny if Kelly needed help. Lots of things.

The talk occasionally turned into ideas of me finding work someday. That was one area that I didn't know what to think. I had learned a lot about what God's word said about women's roles. I fully agreed that women are to be like Proverbs 31 says, the many tasks a mother is to achieve, but at home. Most of those verses, though, say as a *wife.* One problem: I'm not a wife. I'm a single mom who just turned twenty a few weeks ago. Happy, yes, but still living with her parents, no job, getting a small handful of government support for a few baby needs. None of the ladies at church had this worry, so there wasn't anyone there to ask for advice.

Along with all this on my back, I also had concerns about things that weren't really my problems. Friction between my parents was always there. Not so obvious to people outside the family, but those in the family sure saw it. My sister Kelly and her husband weren't seeing eye to eye on too many things. My brother David was having his ups and downs as well. The hardest thing for me, a Christian, knowing God was holding me every day, was that my parents, along with my siblings, did not have that peace. They were going through life without feeling a true, heartfelt need for Christ. Understanding more of that need had me pray for them often, which caused me to cherish my family even more. Sure, it was tough pondering what was the best thing I should, quote, do with my life, unquote, and when I should do whatever that might be, but I had my church family, along with God Himself, helping me feel that peace that passes all understanding.

Journal

June 27, 1987

Cassie Angelyn Houstoun, born March 9 at 11:19 a.m. at Valley General in Renton. Labor was six to seven hours. No pain killer – NATURAL! My favorite person in the whole world. Oh, how she has changed my life. She's almost four months old now, and boy, what a thrill. We're on Welfare, living at home with my parents, and doing very well. I owe it all to my Lord. He has been so generous to us. We are both happy and healthy. My church has been my backbone. I love to see my mom and dad and everyone else love Cassie so much. She, I believe, has brought the smile and laughter back into this household.

God's plan for us is so intense that new areas open up to me daily! I'm now getting my time back enough to do the extra little things I used to do.

As far as a father for Cassie, God has one picked out. I know whom I would choose, of course. Chris Petersen at church. May God's will be done. I now weigh twenty-two pounds less than before I got pregnant! I tell you, it's great to wear things I wore when I was fourteen years old!

I'll end by saying I can't imagine my life without Cassie. I'd give my life for her if I had to. I pray God has chosen her to be called His child.

I don't want to make it sound like life was easy, because it wasn't. Worrying about this, worrying about that, wondering if I should get a job and, if so, where and when, just to name a few things on my plate. But to this day, I am so grateful I wasn't forced by anyone telling me, "You'd better find a job soon." I had total support in hanging low for a bit longer and just loving my daughter. Having my mom and sister around to watch Cassie was something I never took for granted.

Oh, and how dare I not include what my women friends at church, now well aware of how I felt about Chris, would whisper to me? Yes, by this point we ladies frequently talked about the possibilities. "Looks like Chris likes being around your baby," one of them would say while gently bumping up to my shoulder. I loved hearing little comments like that. It was obvious by this point what could—or as I would prefer to think—should start. However, no real sign yet that any solid relationship was forming until...

CHAPTER 13
The Unforgettable Three

"Okay, Willma. Got all your stuff in the car? I'll grab the snacks," I said as she and I gathered our last-minute camping needs together. Camping? Yes. Willma and I had to load the car with things for a little adventure we were going on, taking Cassie with us. That adventure was the first of many once-a-year family camps my church was starting. Wednesday, Thursday, Friday, and Saturday. Three nights, four days of fun, relaxing time, along with a few good messages from a guest speaker. One great summer camp location, indeed. A cabin for each family, plus food, was provided. Pretty much everyone from church was going, and we could invite others to come as well. How could I not invite Willma? A true friend. She came not knowing everyone, but surely knowing I could use some help. She was on her summer break from college and was glad to help me.

When I first heard about this trip, I thought perhaps Cassie was too young to go along. After all, three months is still in the infant category, but as soon as I heard Chris was going, need I say more?

"Golly. Ya know, Willma, I think taking a three-month-old to this should be okay. It would be good for her to get some fresh air." Do you sense an ulterior motive? It took an hour or so of driving to get to a great camping area on this early July day.

Being in a beautiful area, away from our usual hustle-and-bustle surroundings, was so refreshing. But all that was nothing compared to a few things that occurred there. You know when things happen and absolutely nothing in the world can make you forget? Three events during that long weekend fit into that category.

For starters, the first full day was filled with different activities we could all do. Swim, ride little boats, go on the swings, shoot some hoops, and more. My favorite was playing soccer, with enough men and women combined to make two teams. I can picture when Willma and I noticed that Chris had chosen to play.

"Marianne, why don't you play soccer? I'd love to hold Cassie," Willma offered as she winked.

"What a good idea," I said as I returned a wink.

Chris and I were on opposite teams. Shortly after the game started, with all of us adults having fun, Chris and I both wound up going after the ball at the same time. I couldn't help it. "Oops. Sorry," I had to say after I 'accidentally' ran into him. Other players sarcastically said "Oops," also. A few more intentional shoulder-to-shoulder bonks took place if that ball just so happened to be between us. All fun, with loads of laughter. I love soccer.

The next time was the following morning. You can't help but picture the adults and children all needing to get ready for that second breakfast, going in and out of their cabins while taking those little trips to the bathroom all around the same time. I had learned from the morning before how busy it was, so that second morning I knew it was best to get there before anyone else showed up. The earlier, the better. More time alone getting ready to look extra nice.

"Thanks, Willma, for watching Cassie while I go attempt to look presentable," and off I went, not hearing one peep from anyone else at camp. *Oh, good. I must be the only one up and about.*

I stepped out of our room and had to turn right to get to the ladies' room a few doors down. Chris, whose room was on the opposite end, also stepped out of his place, turning left to hit the guys' room a few doors down, right next to the ladies' room. Chris and I, the only ones out, walking straight toward one another.

OH, MY GOODNESS! What a sweet surprise. I think we were both stunned and didn't know what to say. We gave each other a simple good-morning smile. No words, just a smile as six or so seconds walking toward each other took place. Then we got to those restrooms at the same time, opened our own doors, and stepped inside. As soon as I got in, I stared at the mirror. *What. Just. Happened?* I'm convinced God had fun planning that.

The last thing that stood out was, obviously, the best. I'll start by saying that so far, this entire time spent together with Christian friends, hearing great messages, along with Willma helping me watch Cassie, was great. The perfect little escape from my day-to-day life at home. But, sad to say, I did have a wee bit of a cold that last full day. So that, plus the fact that I needed to get up a few times each night for Cassie, had me considering what would be best—to escape for a bit to our little room, away from all the action, taking my baby, my runny nose, and my yawns with me.

"Willma, I'll stay here while Cassie naps after her bottle. You go jump in the pool or whatever sounds fun, if you want." She had helped me so much and was probably glad to go off by herself.

I can still picture that small room. Me lying upon the bed, giving Cassie her bottle, sort of feeling absent from the world. I began, however, to sulk just a little. I remember even wiping a tear or two. Why? Being tired, plus having an irritating runny nose sure didn't help, but added to that I was thinking of all the people out there with all the freedom in the world, being as they didn't have kids, or those who did also had a spouse. Hearing laughter in the distance didn't help how I was feeling. And thoughts of Chris slowly grew. Okay. All right. Thoughts of Chris amplified big time.

I'm sure he's out there chit-chatting away about interesting stuff and having a ball. I'm just here, Miss Mom of a three-month-old, who can't talk about too many interesting things except how to get a perfect bottle ready with your eyes shut at two in the morning. All these thoughts while holding Cassie, who was zonked out in my arms. My precious pillow was right there and I was pondering if I, too, should try to sleep. But my mind was busy and my pillow was getting damp with a few more tears.

Playing soccer the other day or seeing me the other morning probably didn't mean squat to him. I'm sure he's just having fun right now with everyone and probably—.

Suddenly I stopped thinking. It sounded like someone was right outside my slightly opened door.

"Knock, knock," I heard someone quietly say, as I saw a hand holding the door through the opening. "Um, this is Chris. Is... is this your place, Marianne?"

What! Chris is here? Not out with the world? I... I need to wipe my eyes with this blanket. I then saw the most handsome face peeking in, showing a look of uncertainty on what to say.

"Hi, Marianne. Is... is it fine if I'm here? I kinda was wondering where things were and if you might be... just kinda walking around..." or something along those lines. Clearly he wasn't totally sure what he wanted to say.

He was wondering about me. That means he was thinking about me. That's good!

"Oh! Hi!" I knew there was no way anyone would just be walking around in that area at the end of that cabin where our door was. No one. This spot was far away from all the action. He implied a somewhat unclear reason for being away from it all, but, to me, it looked like I was that reason.

"Oh, yes, this is my place. I'm here taking care of Cass. Not doing much. My nose has been bugging me a bit, as you can tell." I had to use that as an excuse if signs of a few tears still showed.

So he stood at the door as I sat on the bed, back against the wall, watching Cassie sleep. I'm sure my pillow was giggling to itself about all of this. We talked about a few things that had stood out those last few days.

"I agree, Chris. The water in the swimming pool is freezing." *By the way, I sure loved 'accidentally' running into you.*

He wasn't there for very long, maybe ten minutes, but during those minutes I went from being Marianne Woe-Is-Me Houstoun to the happiest Houstoun on the planet. Just think, Chris went out of his way, on the farthest-away side of the farthest-away building from all the action, purposefully looking for me. We ended that conversation with some talk of going out there before dinner and doing some of the fun things the others were doing. Well, I needed a couple minutes to touch up, so I said something like, "I need to do a few things with Cassie first. I'll meet you out there shortly. Oh, and thanks for stopping by." He then smiled and slowly closed the door. The rest of that day I just floated. Marianne Happy-As-Could-Be Houstoun.

The next day was Saturday, and knowing we'd all be going our separate ways after breakfast was a bit sad. But another part of me was happy, realizing that maybe, just maybe, something more serious could form between us after those three unforgettable moments. I love camping.

Don't worry. I know we can't picture God, by any means, but I can't help but imagine Him doing something right after Chris and I said, "Goodbye. See ya at church tomorrow." I pictured God kicked back in a nice, plush recliner, His hands up behind His head, giving a small sigh of relief before saying, "These plans of Mine sure are fun."

Remember back when I said I thought how that first time Chris and I saw one another at church, after I visited him with John and Danny as the excuse, was a bit different? Well, seeing each other at church after family camp put that other time to shame. A bit more—oh, too hard to explain. A bit more 'something' was there. Something that caused us to start sitting a wee bit closer during church services. Not right next to each other, mind you. Before the camping trip, he'd be way on the other side of the room or at least quite a few pews back. But not so much now. I usually dropped Cassie off in the nursery before sitting down in my pew before church started, and now Chris would find me and we'd begin talking while waiting for the service to start. That then led him to find a seat in a pew just a few rows back. Nice.

One very special event was now upon us. A few people from church were going to be baptized, and Chris and I were part of that group. I was so thankful for God's hand in saving me and having me go to that church, and I knew I was ready to be baptized. Yes, I was baptized as an infant, having been raised Catholic, but now, knowing the Bible says you must 'repent, believe, and be baptized,' and knowing it was written for it to happen in that order, I knew it meant I was to be baptized again, knowing what took place at that unforgettable camp with Willma a few years earlier, the camp where God opened my eyes to what being a believer truly meant. I would have done it earlier, but something about being pregnant, with a tummy 'out-to-here,' caused me to wait.

We were in line with one other person, waiting for our turns to be baptized. I sure liked thinking that if, Lord willing, God brought us together as husband and wife, how nice it would be to share this memorable occasion of being baptized on the same day.

That night I was filled with thoughts of joy, fulfillment, peace, and love. Thoughts overflowed with how thankful I was of where God had me. I'm sure my pillow felt all that as well. God allowing me to have a perfect four-month-old whom I loved calling all mine; dear friends (one in particular); great messages at church; still having a loving, supportive family at home; me having lost weight; and now, being baptized. I just couldn't ask for more. I felt ready for anything.

The Sunday morning and evening services, plus Wednesday prayer meetings each week, gave Chris and me ample time to visit and get to know more about one another. Mostly talking along with others, but also times when it was just the two of us. Kind of fun hearing one of my lady friends there whisper in my ear, "Marianne, I noticed just you and Chris talking, and I decided to let you two be alone." My way of saying thank you was giving her a big grin.

But one Sunday evening a few weeks after getting back from camping, early July, something stood out. After the service, all the people were chatting for quite a while as usual. Chris was with a few guys over by the wall near the exit door, and I was holding Cassie while talking with a few ladies in another area. Slowly but surely people started to leave. I looked over to see if Chris was still around. (I did that a lot.) As I was grabbing my things to leave, I noticed he was looking right at me even as a man was talking to him. When he noticed I was looking at him, he instantly made the come-here hand signal.

WHAT? He wants ME to come over THERE? First time any request like this has ever happened. Holding Cassie, I slowly began heading toward him. I can still picture exactly where he was standing. The man he was talking to got the clue that Chris had to talk to me about something and said, "Oh, that's fine. I'll tell you the rest later."

"Thank you," Chris told him. "I just need to talk to her before she heads out."

WHAT? He has something just for me to hear? First time for that too.

With me finally there, he said, "Marianne, where I work, we have two special work gatherings a year. Usually a nice dinner somewhere. One's around Christmas and the other one's in the summer. Most everyone that works there brings someone. Well..."

Did I just hear right? No. This must be a dream.

"...I was wondering if you would like to go with me? I know it's short notice, but it's this next Saturday. Would... would you like to?"

Would I LIKE to? Perfect time for that well-known saying, 'Do dogs bark?'

Trying my hardest to seem calm, "I... I don't see any reason why not. I'm sure my mom could watch Cassie."

He then gave a few details about it, but I'm sure I was thinking more about if this was really happening or if I was just having a dream.

"Let's see. I don't think I have your phone number handy. Here, let me write it down," he said while finding his pen. "I don't know the exact time of it, but I'll call and tell you when I'd pick you up if... if that's okay."

"Yes, that should be fine." *He's going to call me? I love telephones.* So glad there wasn't texting back then.

I will admit, to this day I remember what my main thoughts were as I began walking toward the door to leave. *I can't believe it. He asked me out. I can't believe it. But... but what should I wear?*

And, because of that thought, as soon as I got home, after telling my mom and after putting Cassie to bed, I went through all the clothes in my closet while still grinning from ear to ear. I ended that day with an important decision: *I'm getting a new dress first thing in the morning.*

My pillow surely could sense something exciting had happened as it soaked in my many thoughts. *I can't believe it. I can't believe it.* That pillow sensed a side of me it had never noticed before. And not just thoughts, but now prayer.

God, please may You be starting something that's right. Something that's best for me and Cassie and, of course, Chris. Thank You so much for having him want to ask me. And on and on and on, my pillow soaked it up. Those were the final thoughts my pillow was hearing before I finally fell asleep. Wait, I take that back. I do believe my last thought was, *Now what time does that store open?*

CHAPTER 14
Picture Perfect

If I had all the time in the world to write and you had all the time in the world to read, then I'd be sharing with you every little detail of what happened the night of our first date. But since neither of us has all the time in the world, I'll keep it short and sweet.

I was all ready, having finished, quote, 'doing my hair,' still hoping I had chosen the right dress to wear. My mom was holding Cassie as we heard Chris's car drive up.

"He's here," I said, even though I knew we had both heard his car come to a stop. The best car-parking sound I had ever heard. My mom was so happy to finally meet the man I talked so much about.

Knock, knock.

I learned that night that when you hear a perfect knock, a knock at your front door, and then you open that door and see a really handsome twenty-three-year-old who says hello the best way imaginable, and then says it just as perfectly to your mom, you can't help but leave the house thinking it's all just a dream. Note: comparing that first time saying hello to my mom to someone ELSE'S first time saying hello to my mom, you can understand why I might say this one was perfect.

Now don't worry, I didn't let those first few minutes convince me that there wouldn't be any glitches that evening. I didn't instantly think he was the best man in the world, but I did know for certain he was the best man in my driveway on that dead-end street in Normandy Park. It was only a few seconds after we left that he proved even more I was right. He opened his car's passenger door for me. As he walked around to the driver's door, I thought at least two—no, make that three hundred times, *He opened my door! He opened my door!*

Now this being written thirty years after it happened, I don't remember perfectly everything we talked about. I know he told me more about his work, those he works with, and what to expect when meeting them. What I do remember for sure, though, is that it was the best twenty-minute conversation I'd ever had with someone in a car. When we got to the place and parked, he swiftly got out to let me know he would open the door for me. *He opened my door again!*

So here we are, going into a nice conference building. This handsome man guiding me toward his coworkers' reserved area. Men and women, all dressed up, standing around talking to one another. I then realized I'd never done anything like this before. Nervous as I was, I do believe that I hid it rather well and soon felt comfortable. *I so hope I will be seeing these people at the next gathering, and the next and the next and the next.*

When someone at our table asked, "So what do you do for work?" I did share about my daughter, but even then I kept my reply, "I stay home with my five-month-old daughter" sweet and simple. I think people knew it wasn't an appropriate time to give all the soap-opera details about being a single mother. Instead, "Oh, how sweet. Such an adorable age," or the like was heard.

Dinner was great. The atmosphere was great. But the best part was the man sitting next to me.

After dinner we all went on a Lake Washington sightseeing cruise for a few hours. Picture a spectacular summer evening out on a large beautiful boat, looking out at the lake with a Mr. Chris Petersen by your side. *Okay, clock. Please stop right now for, oh, six hours or so.* But, sad to say, the clock didn't stop. Time for the boat ride to end. As we stepped back onto land, I remember thinking how sad I was because I knew that meant the gathering of fellow workers was over, so time to go back home. Darn it. I didn't want it to end. It felt like we had just left my house to start this night, but in reality, we were getting in the car for him to take me back to my house. (And yes, he opened the door for me again.)

Our last twenty or so minutes were underway, and we reminisced about the dinner, the people there, and the boat ride. He also shared a bit more about the few difficulties he'd had working with unbelievers, along with a few other situations that don't really fit the chit-chatting-at-church category.

By the time we got to my house, I felt we had passed the 'just-friends' zone. Having gone out to an important dinner, plus having talked about a few more serious things, sure had me thinking, *I'm so glad I bought this dress.* But not just that. *Chris is one true gentleman. I can easily say that this entire evening really has been a perfect dream.*

I'll tell you right now, part of me knows you're wondering one particular thing. No, no goodnight kiss. He did, however, open the door for me to get out and did walk me to the front door. We ended the night by saying a few of those common, but unforgettable, words.

"I had a good time this evening. So glad you could come."

"Thank you, Chris, for asking. I had a really nice time too."

And after that, probably said in unison, "See you at church tomorrow."

When I walked in my house, everyone was already asleep. Perfect, too, because I didn't want to talk. I didn't want a conversation that could take my thoughts away from that seemingly perfect evening. I take that back. I did talk to someone else: God. While lying down on my pillow, smiling ear to ear, God heard me thank Him for what felt like, to me, a dream come true. But, of course, the practical side of me was also there. (Darn it.)

There is a thought I've used for years now that I do believe started that night. That thought? Assume the worst but hope for the best. Yes, I overflowed with hopes and sure loved thinking of the best outcome from that night, yet still thought it would be good to assume that this wasn't going to work out. But overall, my pillow was detecting one happy woman.

That night being a Saturday meant the next morning was church! Remember how the first time I saw him at church after I had taken my two nephews to visit him was a speck more special than all those times before? Or how that Sunday after he and I spent time at family camp was even more special? But now, after an official date, words can't explain. Maybe no one else around us could tell, but I sure could. I could tell from that look, that look between us, that we were no longer just friends.

A three-word phrase began that day: Chris and Marianne. From that point on we began sitting closer during church, which led us to talking a lot more after the service. After I'd get Cassie from the nursery immediately after church ended, Chris and I would often wind up being among the last ones to leave. I was thankful Cassie was so little, about five – to six-months old, so I didn't need to chase her here and there. Nope. I got to stand, hold Cassie, and talk to Chris more about serious, fun, practical, or even silly things. But what was really great was talking about spiritual things. Hearing and talking about the same messages was so beneficial. I could tell it was a blessing to be getting to know a Christ-centered young man who was, by the way, gorgeous.

Now, if you remember, Chris lived a good twenty-five-minutes' distance, if no traffic, at his little basement rental near the University of Washington. At church we had a Sunday morning and evening service, so between services he often stayed in the area at one of the guys from church's homes. He'd bring some extra things like clothes, books, and whatnot for the full day. It became his Sunday ritual.

A few Sundays after that dreamy evening out, Chris, myself, and a few others were talking after the morning service.

"Hmmm," Chris said. "The guys I usually go home with between services have something else going on." While looking around, he continued, "Just seeing who else I might go hang out with today."

ME, ME, ME, ME, ME!

"Well, um, Cassie and I are just going home. No plans. If you want to come on over, it's fine by me."

PLEASE, PLEASE, PLEASE SAY YES.

"Why, thanks, Marianne. If you're sure it's no problem."

"It's handy living close to church," I said as we walked together toward our cars. "Glad I can help. Just follow me. It's really close."

I decided in the car that I would hold Cassie for a while after getting home. I wasn't sure how spending about four or so hours at my house with him and my parents would go, so keeping Cassie with me, all sweet and lovable, meant we would at least have something cute to talk about.

My mom grinned big time as we came inside.

"Mom, Chris sorta needed a place to hang out today. I'll make lunch for us."

"Well, hi, Chris. Nice to see you again. Oh, Marianne, I insist. Let me just whip something together for you both," she said, grinning ear to ear. (I love my mom.)

"I'm just running upstairs to change, plus change Cassie's diaper. I'll be right down. There's the bathroom, since you brought clothes as well," I said before going upstairs. I did give myself an extra look in the mirror before I came back down after changing into my nicer kick-back attire than I usually changed into after church.

It wasn't as long as I thought, not even fifteen minutes, before I said, "Time for Cassie to go have her nap." That was probably one of the fastest bottles I gave her, and then put her down for the longest nap I probably ever hoped she'd have.

Now, I can't promise a hundred percent correct memory of that afternoon, but I do know we went outside on the back deck to eat. Time to picture that perfect scene from a movie where beautiful music is playing while watching a young man and woman sitting outside on a back porch on a dazzling sunny afternoon, seeing them talking back and forth, taking turns eating while listening as the other one talks. Both smiling, occasionally laughing, with perhaps an older woman coming out a time or two to bring more lemonade. Picture perfect, don't ya think?

We talked and talked and talked and, when done, walked down to the creek on our property so he could finally see this place he'd heard so much about. We came back inside after a while and had a conversation with both my parents. A nice conversation, us four. Time spent, too, in the front yard, and, with Chris working as a landscape architect, I could tell Mom enjoyed showing off all the flowers here and there, soaking in the facts about them that Chris shared. Cassie was up after a while, and I loved showing him all her little baby toys and whatnot around.

One of the fastest afternoons between services had just taken place. All Sunday-afternoon hours before this day took forever while waiting to see Chris again, but that Sunday? A hundred-and-eighty-degree turn. *This Sunday it's too fast!*

The clock told us it was time to think of heading back to church. Four hours spent sharing past experiences, present goals, and future hopes, and how God was guiding us through it all, was now needing to end.

"Glad I could help today with somewhere for you to hang out. It'll take me a bit to get ready."

"Yeah," he said. "Might be best if I just head out now and see you at church." He grabbed his things and thanked me again while getting into his car. The only good thing about seeing him take off was that I'd see him again in about thirty minutes back at church.

Once I got out of the car at church, a few of the ladies simply grinned at me, knowing about the company I'd had that afternoon. I'm sure some who didn't know were probably thinking, "Why does she look so happy?"

CHAPTER 15
Peeking in My Journal

Watching this baby grow, amazed at all the joy she has brought to me and my family, and knowing I had written so much in *my* journal about her, I decided I wanted to have her read her very own journal someday. When she gets older, I want her to read how she brought so much joy into my life from day one. So I began a new journal, just for her.

Cassie's Journal-

August 2, 1987

How does one even start to write down what one feels inside about the gift that God has so graciously given? God has granted me the most beautiful daughter I could ever hope for. I guess I'm writing this journal so that when she asks me years from now, "Why do you love me?" or "What's it like having a baby?" I'll be able to give this to her to read. I'm starting this almost five months after she was born, but I remember it as if it were yesterday. The joy increases as each day passes. She is growing like a weed and is learning so many things. She is, however, crying right now, wanting me to turn off the bedroom lights so she and I can go to sleep. Goodnight.

August 4, 1987

As I watch Cassie lying on her back in her crib, trying to tap the plastic toys hanging above her head with her hairless doll, I could just cry with the thought of losing her. I get these scary thoughts of someone taking her from me and me having no idea where she is. Lord, I pray nothing like that happens. Watching her get control of her body is so entertaining! She rolled from her back to her stomach today!! She pooped in her bath the other day, too. How could I not write that down? Her sucking her toes is a good pastime, too. Cassie just loves them.

August 10, 1987

How I praise God for giving me a little girl. I wanted one so badly. I guess mostly because I felt it would be easier on me, being her only parent for now. Oh, how I pray God gives her a father who will love her as his own. God has carried us through thus far; I don't think He will stop now.

August 17, 1987

Today in Safeway a man asked me which aisle I found the baby on. Funny guy. Chris Petersen sent Cassie a letter through the mail. Her very first letter! The front was a cover of what should be a magazine. The title: INFANT. Then it listed the supposed articles that would be in the magazine. For instance, Are Rattles Passe? and How to Break the Ice at Nursery, and Ten New Things to Cry About. On the other side are sweet words from him to her. I think Cassie is falling for him.

By this point Chris had been around Cassie quite often. It slowly became a sweet assumption that he'd come to my house each Sunday between church services. I'll never forget the first time Chris suggested he drive all three of us to my house in his car. Heck, why waste gas, right? We stopped by a Denny's restaurant on the way. It was our first time going somewhere for no specific reason. Chris, myself, and Cassie, sitting at that table, when whoever was serving us would give the oh-what-a-cute-baby comment. That was the first time he paid for our food. Sort of felt like some official something. To this day I still remember how, when we went to the counter to pay, he shared his debit card number with me. That means a lot, don't ya think? *Oh, he told me his pin number. 1779. I love this number.*

As you may remember, my journal showed much peace and joy while I was in this not-so-perfect situation as a single mom. Cherishing my little girl sure helped me feel better, even with the not-so-great family affairs going on. I do admit I felt a bit spoiled compared to problems I knew others had to deal with. I was seeing how rare it was for someone in my shoes to have it so easy.

I had heard stories of other young single moms who had things much tougher than me, such as extremely hard deliveries, fighting day in and day out with the baby's father, the mom's parents being difficult, plus weight gain, no friends, having to work and live on their own. I'm sure many more tough situations could be put on that list.

I often pondered then how it could have been for me. What if I had married Greg? What if my parents were like some of the parents who say, "You did it; you deal with it"? And what about those who didn't have support from a church family? But, worst of all, what if I didn't believe in and trust God? I don't know how I would have turned out if I didn't. Actually, I do know. I'd feel lost.

It might look like I was the happiest single mom on the planet. Sometimes I felt I was, but I still had worries and wishes, along with my own selfishness. Sure, I could pass time staring at Cassie and thinking about Chris. Sure, I could feel somewhat spoiled at how easy things did seem to be for me then. Sure this, sure that.

But there were still what-if-this and what-if-that thoughts floating around too. What if I hadn't gone to California? What if I had continued on with college courses, finally learning the right skills to make my dream of making movies come true? What if I had followed the right path in meeting Mr. Wonderful, falling in love, getting married, and *then* having my first child?

Being the only single mom at church was not that odd anymore. But I did have some hidden thoughts as I saw a few other ladies about to have their first babies with their husbands right there by their sides. Often at night, lights out, with Cassie sound asleep, I would lie in bed, pillow and all, and think about these things. My pillow could still sense a bit of worry, feeling the weight of my many what-if or should-have or I-want thoughts. *If I found a job, who would watch Cassie? If my parents ever did decide to separate, who would I stay with? Should I go back to school? Should I make a goal and plan to be out of this house by a certain month?* How much easier if I just had to think of myself. I'm sure you could add to these yourself. Yes, God and my pillow could feel my overflowing questions.

During the day it wasn't so bad. I stayed busy caring for Cassie, doing work around the house, running a few errands here and there, occasionally babysitting Kelly's boys, watching TV (smiling each time I heard a certain name on that certain soap opera), or just relaxing and chatting with my mom while we sat outside on the porch swing. So, thankfully, the days were more positive. But come most evenings, alone on my bed, I prayed for God's help and guidance. Even if I didn't feel like praying, I still knew He was there for me, just as my pillow was right there as well. I didn't share these nighttime thoughts in my journal much at all, but, as you'll see, it's just because I had better things to write about.

My Journal

October 5, 1987

Oh, my, oh, my. For starters, Cassie is now almost

seven months. WOW. She's almost got her crawling mastered, and boy, can she scoot! She's such a charmer now too. God has truly blessed me with a very healthy, beautiful baby. I'm still a full-time mommy, which is fine with me.

CHAPTER 16
Fast Forward to Reality

As the main purpose for this book is to encourage those going through an unplanned pregnancy, I am now going to fast forward about six months. Why? I'm assuming you are not reading this because you're in need of a gigantic love story.

First, let me tell you a bit more of what I discovered about Chris as this relationship was forming. He was not looking for a relationship when he began going to church. No preconceived plans of finding Ms. Right, becoming a daddy a few years later, while living on a picture-perfect dead-end street where everyone waves at each other when driving up. But no opposite plan of being single forever either. He knew it was best to spend any extra time studying for school and studying God's word. His job working in a landscape architect firm also took time. Occasionally he visited his parents, his older brother or older sister and her family, as they all lived fairly close by. So all of that came first, followed closely by mastering the nuking of frozen store-bought meals just right. After all, he was a bachelor.

But as those first few months went by, Chris got used to me as a mom, with my precious daughter in my arms, with that necessary bottle close at hand. I guess you could say Cassie's cuteness caught Chris's heart. It became somewhat normal seeing the three of us blending together rather smoothly. You can safely assume that Chris and I, being the only single adults at church, spent more time talking as the weeks and months went by. Everyone at church knew we weren't just friends anymore.

I'll never forget one Sunday evening. He and I were talking as the last people were leaving. I was holding Cassie, who must have been about six months old then. "Okay, guys," said one of the men, "time I lock up. Out we go."

Chris and I were not done talking, so as those last few people drove off, we continued our conversation while standing outside the main-entrance door. Time again for the perfect song in the background as you watch us, me holding my sleeping baby. It was obvious neither one of us wanted to end the evening, even though everyone had left and the sun was beginning to set. On that beautiful night, we sat down on top of the stairs.

– Story time

"Marianne, it's getting a bit cooler. Here, since Cassie's sleeping, let me put my jacket around your shoulders." (Now remember, you're hearing beautiful music as you picture all this.) Sitting down right next to each other at the top of the stairs, sensing this was more than your typical conversation, he placed his jacket around her and kept his arm around her shoulder as they talked. The first occurrence of any physical contact that really meant anything. The scene now shows night, a few outside lights shining brightly. Two lovebirds, side by side, smiling, talking, her holding the baby while his arm is around her. The camera slowly moves away, romantic music playing as the scene fades.

Okay, back to reality.

When did the title of lovebirds become more official? A few weeks after that movie took place, there was one early evening at the end of summer, just as he was leaving my house, I said, "Oh, wait. I'll be right back. There's something I forgot to give you," and back inside I went. You see, I felt like giving him a batch of the cookies I made that day for my family. Okay, I lied. I made them for him but did at least leave a few in the kitchen for my parents. Anyway, I put them in a shoebox and even went the extra mile and covered that box with the comics that came in the Sunday papers. Heck, why not?

Back outside again. "Here ya go. I made some cookies and thought you might like to take some with you."

He was stunned. I'll never forget that look on his face. He was at a loss for words. He looked at the box now in his hand, then at me, then the box, and then at me for a second or two, followed by slowly coming closer, giving me the best short, sweet, simple first kiss. Our friendship had instantly changed.

"No one's really made cookies for me before. Thank you," he said while looking at me, then the box, then back at me.

He. Just. Kissed. Me. I just made cookies thinking he'd like them. Not that he'd kiss me. I'm sure glad I made them.

"You're welcome." The smile on both our faces said it all. No longer just friends.

"See you Sunday."

"Bye, Chris." I said while floating.

I love cookies.

Time now to fast forward.

That first kiss gave us the okay to start a serious relationship. There were a few other signs showing that he was more than a typical boyfriend.

Sign one: Remember how I told you all the other guys asked me why my hands were so wrinkly? On one unforgettable day, as Chris and I sat at the kitchen table—yes, another one of those events where you remember every little detail—I was holding something small up close for him to see, which also allowed him to see my hands.

"What is it with your skin on your hands?"

Here we go.

"Looks like it's covered with diamonds."

WHAT? DIAMONDS? He said DIAMONDS? DIAMONDS on my hands instead of wrinkles! Did I just die and go to heaven? I knew right then and there that he was the man I was destined to marry.

Sign two: It took place at that Denny's on that first drive together to my house after church. You know, that 1779 debit-number lunch. After being seated, the waitress asked if we'd like some coffee. At the same time we both answered, "No, thank you." We stared at each other.

"You don't like coffee either?" and on we gabbed how we each felt like we were the only ones in Seattle who didn't like coffee.

He's it.

Sign three: The best sign that things were heading in the right direction. Remember the Cove, the place my song "Parked at the Cove" came from? Well, one evening sitting by a little campfire down at the Cove after the sun had gone down, those three words were finally exchanged. I love you.

My Journal

October 7, 1987
Can't hold it back. For the first time in my life I have found—or should I say—God has given me the man I pray to spend the rest of my life with. Heavy sounding, I know, but oh, so true. Praise God! We've been doing a lot of stuff together and both of us were struggling with our feelings toward each other. Then the Lord revealed a love between us. One great night at the Cove we exchanged "I love you," and one month later it is still strong. He has one year left at the university in Landscape Architecture. He's such a godly man and wants to follow Christ. That is my biggest attraction to him.

(I think you can tell I was floating.)

The time came for me to meet his parents, and that day was unforgettable. Chris and I, carrying Cassie, who at this point was about seven months old, walked into their home. I felt an instant welcome. Instant comfort. Instant sincere warmth being shown to us both. The thoughts I drenched my pillow with that night? *He has great parents. One great set of in-laws they sure could be.*

Winter was now close at hand. People at church, along with my family, knew that Chris and I were head over heels in love with each other. Chris and Marianne, two names glued together. Of course, no one dared ask if we were thinking of getting married, but if you could read people's minds, most were wondering that.

I do need to share, however, how we were not one of those couples who openly talked about marriage. No 'someday if we get married' or 'when we get married we should live...' Nope, not once. Even after sharing all the I love yous back and forth for a few months, both agreeing how thankful we were that God had brought us together, we just didn't get into any conversation about marriage.

Proof. One day toward the end of November, he had to get something in Lamonts, the nicer clothing store in town. While I held Cassie, we walked in, chatting about what type of socks he needed to find. There it was, as soon as we walked in. You've all seen one. A huge, shiny glass table with twenty million engagement rings all screaming, LOOK AT US! LOOK AT US!

There is absolutely no way in the world I could forget what happened when we saw all those rings. We had been completely relaxed, happy-go-lucky, and then, BANG, saw them. We both instantly turned our heads a bit to the right as if we never noticed them, each of us drowning in thoughts like, *OH, NO! Wedding rings! EEK!* or *Wedding rings mean we might need to talk about getting married,* or *We don't say the 'M' word, so can't look at the 'W' rings, because we'd then probably wind up talking about getting M-A-R-R-I-E-D.*

Since we had to walk straight toward those rings before getting near the clothes, we just acted all relaxed, yet secretly thinking, *Man, this is weird,* while stepping past them a hair faster than normal, heads turned while saying, "Now, where do they keep those socks?"

CHAPTER 17
Learning Reality the Hard Way

December. A few weeks later.

These have been the best six months I have pretty much ever had. Mistletoe, where are you?

December marked Cassie—the most special person to me in the entire universe—now being nine months old. Nine months of having the privilege of staying home, being able to witness the first in everything with her.

December, however, also marked the time I learned something very important. Don't get your hopes up. Don't assume that the light at the end of the tunnel will automatically be the light you think it is. Yes, God does what is best for His children, but what He plans may not be exactly what *we* think is best.

As Chris and I built this relationship, we were both growing closer to God as well. Put the two together and I was thinking we were ready to say 'I do,' ready to pledge our forever-lasting love to one another.

You know what that means: you can't stop thinking about it. That last week of November I was drowning in thoughts. *We are ready to not only say 'I love you,' but also 'I do.' And I bet he's thinking the same thing.* And you know what really triggered me thinking that? The day we walked into Lamonts. I mean, how could I NOT think more along those lines after all those rings hollered out "GET MARRIED!"

He must be thinking about it. No way was he only thinking about

*socks when we saw those rings. He MUST be! Will he ask me?
When will he ask me? were my thoughts twenty-four/seven.*

I then began convincing myself he was on the same wavelength, since that's all I was thinking about aside from when to change a diaper, fill a bottle, or how to master smooshing up bananas to feed Cassie. Night after night for a good week, while trying to sleep, darkness all around me, my pillow time took over. Thoughts overflowing of Chris, me, and us together.

He must be planning to ask me soon. After all, we love each other, he's almost done with college, plus he'll stay working where he works now. Why NOT? No real excuse to wait!

I had convinced myself he would ask.

Christmas Day? New Year's Eve? New Year's Day? Maybe at Cassie's first birthday party come March? Nah, too long. He'll ask sooner than that, I bet.

One of those nights, my pillow felt a major earthquake when I put two and two together. After I convinced myself he wanted to ask me, I realized his work's holiday dinner was to be the following Saturday. *THAT'S IT! PERFECT! Perfect time for him to ask me. That's GOTTA be when he will.* It was like fireworks going off in my head.

My pillow must have thought, "Oh, great. She's going crazy again," but I didn't mind. I decided right then and there that he would ask me that night. No real excuse not to. We would be one dashing dressed-up duo, with a holiday-ish Christmas feel all around. How could he not ask me on such a perfect night? *After all, our first real date was at the summer dinner. It would be perfect to be asked to marry him the night of the company's Christmas dinner. He must be thinking the same thing. But maybe he's not. No, he's got to! He will.*

Questions began to form.

1) Will he ask? Yes.

2) What day will he ask? The evening of his work's holiday dinner.

3) How will he ask? Hey, I don't know everything.

And more. Will he ask while driving to the dinner and have a planned love song come on the radio first before asking? Will he do the traditional get on his knees and ask while outside as the perfect moonlight shines on us? (Ignoring how cold it would be, being it *was* December.) Or will he, during the dinner, stand up, tap the wine glass, and ask all to witness him asking the most important question of his life? *Wake up, Marianne. Shake your head and just be happy any way he asks.*

The night before, my pillow could sense a little bit of my worry. *But... but what if he doesn't ask?* But that thought wasn't there for long at all. I just knew he would. *How will he ask? How should I answer? Will he have a ring?*

I didn't think I'd be able to fall asleep, but somehow I did. That next morning I'm sure even Cassie could tell I was a bit different. If she could talk, she would have asked, "Mommy, why are you staring into outer space more than normal today? I want more applesauce."

Hours slowly went by.

This dress or that dress? I'll test my makeup one more time after I try that dress on first. I have to look perfect when he asks. Yes, a basket case.

That night was also a bit different for me because his car–I forget what exactly–was having a problem, so I had to drive out to his place. But he would be the one driving it to the restaurant.

"Bye, Mom. Thanks again for watching Cassie," I said while giving Cassie a smooch goodbye. *This is the last time you will see me not engaged.*

I sang my heart away while listening to my favorite tape full of love songs, but the closer I got to his place, the calmer I got while contemplating the best way to say yes.

When will he ask me? As soon as he sees me? In the car? During dinner? Before we get back to the car? I know. Save the best for last and ask when we get back to his place.

As I drove up and opened the door to get out, my thoughts

quickly changed. *MY HAIR'S GETTING WET!* There was a light drizzle that night, of all nights. As I knocked on the door to let him know I, Marianne Mastered-At-How-To-Say-Yes Houstoun, was there—no texting to let him know I was staying dry in the car waiting—I felt totally ready for this awesome evening. Wet, but ready.

The door opened and there he was, Mr. Wearing-A-Tie, all ready to go. With water coming down, we gave each other a really quick kiss, I gave him my key, and faster than normal we walked to the car.

There. Sitting in the car. *Now?*

He turned the key. *Nope, not now.*

Then we started our usual talking while driving. He shared a few things that would be discussed at the restaurant, company-talk. I told him how the last few days had been, and, as normal, the adorable things Cassie had done as well. Back and forth, back and forth. Again, a nice drive with Chris.

We got there.

I know. As soon as we step out he might say something like, "I can't wait to ask you—" or better yet, maybe inside he'll do the "Excuse me, everyone," while standing up as everyone is eating. Yeah, that's it. He'll say, "I need to ask the love of my life if she will—" That's

PERFECT!

Wrong. Neither one happened.

Eating and visiting were still great. Talking with people I had talked with six months earlier was enjoyable, and seeing how the company's owner gave out awards was also nice to witness. When all that was coming to an end, I thought how Chris really wasn't one of those types who would ask me to marry him in front of tons of people. After all, that event was for the company, not us.

Silly me. Why did I even think he should have done it then? Time now to head back to his place. Not much time left for him to ask. I know! Maybe he'll surprise me and make one last stop at a special place before going back to his place! That's it. He'll get down on one knee, pull out a ring, and ask.

Nope.

Soon, after talking about the good food, awards, and more about the people, the front door of his place could be seen, since the windshield wipers were doing their job.

The car stopped. *This is it. It's gotta be now.*

"I so much would like you to come in for a bit, but..." he said.

But I love you so much and can't wait another second. Will you marry me?

Here he goes!

"...but I have this deadline for school tomorrow that I have to spend tons of time on tonight. I know if you came in for a little bit, I wouldn't want you to leave, and therefore wouldn't get any studying done."

Wait, what did I just hear? That's nothing close to what I expected.

"I'm so sorry, but I really should just force myself to say goodnight here. You understand, right? I would so love it if you could come in, but..."

"Oh, don't you worry. It was so nice going tonight," I said with a totally fake smile. *I can't believe this. I CANNOT believe this.*

We both had to get out while the rain was pouring down, pass each other a quick goodbye kiss and share our 'I love you' to each other. I then zoomed quickly to the driver's side and got in. He looked at me, standing by the door, waving, while I looked at him with a phony ear-to-ear grin.

I can't believe this. I just CANNOT believe this.

So there I was, wet, in my car, driving away. What in the world was I to do? Go to some bar to try to escape life for a while? Of course not. How about I just wake up with my pillow screaming to me "Marianne, GET UP! You're having a terrible nightmare!" Nope. It was just a time I drove all by myself in the car, on a rainy night, with a few tears mixing with the rain on my cheeks.

I can't believe it. I thought for sure he'd ask me tonight. My mind began swelling up with thoughts. *But why didn't he? No reason in the world not to ask me, so maybe... maybe he... doesn't ever want to ask me!*

And after that thought, those few tears turned into a waterfall. Glad it was pouring down rain and the windows were all fogged up so no one on the freeway could see my tears or hear me bawling that night while driving.

Why? Why doesn't he want to marry me? WHY? My thoughts overflowed just like my tears.

I knew he wasn't feeling at all strange or unnatural in having a serious relationship with someone who had a child. We both felt that unforgettable first kiss meant we were ready to have a serious relationship. And the more time Chris, Cassie, and I spent together, a special love grew among the three of us. So Chris adjusting to getting involved with a woman who was also a mother seemed to come naturally to him. It was obvious in words and action how thankful he was God had brought us together. So why he didn't want to marry me? I couldn't help but wonder.

I'm ugly. I have too cute of a baby. Maybe he thinks that he's too cute for me or... or maybe he's too weak to tell me he wants to break up. Maybe I'm not Christian enough for him or he doesn't like driving my car. I was trying to think of anything about myself that I needed to fix. After all those thoughts, one small fact hit me, and it hit me hard as if a tiny bullet was shot right in the middle of my forehead. I left God out.

Things were going so sweet those last three or four weeks that I just put God to the side. Life for Marianne Life-Is-Sweet Houstoun was going exceptionally well, and I didn't feel a need for any help. Sort of an all's-fine-and-dandy phase, and I felt I could just do what I thought was needed to keep it that way. My pillow probably savored that calm, peace-filled head of mine. Thoughts of Chris and me, him playing with Cassie, he and I always sitting next to each other at church. It all made up for Cassie not yet sleeping perfectly through the night. Life was great! I was too busy thinking to myself how nice it all was and not really even thinking about, or thanking, God.

So I'm in the car, about halfway home, and the tears are no longer pity-party tears but now tears of guilt, realizing how I had left God out of the picture.

God, I'm sorry. I'm sorry I thought only about how he should be asking me. I'm sorry I made it seem like he is what my life is to be centered around and that I need him more than I need You. I'm wrong. It's You and only You I should be needing right now. I shouldn't need Chris. I need You.

My thoughts were going in a bit of a different direction on those remaining miles home.

God, help me, please. From now on I will assume it's just me and the daughter You gave me, in Your hands; no one else. I will focus on what I need to do as her mom. I will assume, for now, that I will not get married and that Chris and I will not work out and will soon end this relationship. If he is keeping me from walking with You, focusing on You, then I should set him aside and be content to have only You holding me and Cassie. I'll focus on getting a job and starting a new life outside my parents' house, trusting You will guide me. No more staying there till I get married. It won't be easy, but I know You will help me somehow, someway.

I never forgot that part of my drive. Still feels like yesterday. The saying 'let go and let God' fit perfectly right then and there. I felt I needed to let go of my own desires, my own plans for myself, and instead focus on God's plans for me. Those last few minutes of my drive I pondered on how the last few weeks had been more me and Chris instead of me and Christ.

I slowly pulled up the driveway, hoping all the rain would hide that obvious tear-drenched look I knew would show as I walked in. *PLEASE, no one be up.* Talk about being relieved. I sure was, being both my parents were in bed. A quick stop in the bathroom and an even quicker look in the mirror. To this day I don't recall ever seeing my face so stained with tears. I went straight to my room, got into my pj's, but only after checking on Cassie. How could I not look at her a bit longer than usual, having just realized that she and Christ, not Chris, were now the main two I'd focus on?

Time to escape it all under my blanket and on my pillow. Perfect darkness. My pillow sure noticed a difference in me that night compared to those many nights before. I wasn't filling it with thoughts about Chris and me or how he'll ask me to marry him. Instead, that pillow could tell something was wrong, as it was getting a bit damp.

But that time, while crying, my pillow sensed my thoughts changing. As minutes went by, a new feeling began to show. Feeling a little more at peace thinking about Chris, but with a 't.' That's all. Much more peace when I put Christ first, enough so that I managed to finally end those tears and fall asleep.

Yes, I still loved Chris. And I knew it was true love and felt he did love me. But knowing God loved me more than Chris did, I knew I needed to love Him more in return. Honor, obey, respect, and love God above all else. My new reality.

CHAPTER 18
New Beginning — New End

So, are you curious how I was feeling when I woke up the next morning? Let's see how long of a list I can make to help describe it. Sad, happy, angry, selfish, loved, helpless, courageous, devoted, worn out, excited, reinforced, along with miserable, empty, terrified, and, of course, curious how I'd look after staying up most of the night flooding my pillow with thoughts galore.

The one word I wasn't feeling that morning was lonely. I knew I wasn't alone. A little like before, when God pulled me out of that entire mess with Greg, using a long walk with Eyde and Willma as His tool. Not that I felt God was far away before this great awakening, but just that He was closer now. Oh, it's hard to explain.

There was another way I felt once I held Cassie that morning, I felt a new mother-daughter connection. Now, mind you, I hadn't lost that feeling before those last twelve hours, but just something about holding her that morning was somewhat of a new beginning for me. I'm sure I stayed in my room until she woke up. I'd rather my mom's first words by the fireplace to be "Come here to Grandma, you cutie pie," instead of, "So how was last night?"

But, of course, I couldn't avoid my mom asking that at some point. "It was good meeting more people he works with. And the food was great." Sweet and simple. No way would I explain all the turmoil my mind had gone through that night. Only my pillow and God needed to know. No one could have understood anyway, so why even try to explain?

That entire day I was rather calm, quiet, and collected, entangled with many thoughts, yet at peace. My assume-the-worst-but-hope-for-the-best thinking continued to form. I was assuming this relationship would not really lead to marriage, but I hoped for the best, that someday it would.

Ring, ring. Ring, ring.

Of course, back then we weren't spoiled like we are now with phones that can tell us who's calling. You can probably guess what I was thinking. *Chris. I bet that's Chris.* Part of me didn't want to answer it, but the other side of me knew I should. I forget if I answered it or if my mom did, but I was right.

God's first, Cassie's next. God's first, Cassie's next.

"Hi, Chris."

"Hi, Marianne," he said. "Hope driving home was okay with it raining so much."

Rain? Rain wasn't my problem last night. "Oh, it was fine."

He continued on, saying he was sorry I had to just drop him off, and wanted to see if we'd like to try to see each other again that evening. We had tentatively planned to get together again in a few days, but nothing certain.

"I got quite a bit of studying done, and I think I did pretty good with that test. How about we get together tonight? Nothing fancy like last night, of course. I'm still without a car, so you and Cassie could come over here."

Believe it or not, I liked that idea. He was always over at my place, so I thought this little change was good.

Heck, a change of scenery to go along with the change of my thoughts.

"Sure! Sounds good."

A few hours followed with more happy, yet confusing, thoughts swirling through my mind. However, most of them were focused on Cassie and the life she and I would have. *I've got a new life now as a mom. Come on, brain. Just focus on Cassie and God.*

It sure was easier getting ready to head out that night compared to the night before. Simpler clothes, simpler face, plus the weather was so much better. After getting Cassie in the car and pulling out of the driveway, my thoughts led to prayer. Praying for God to help guide my heart for the evening ahead. While driving on that same freeway as the night before, I couldn't help but look at cars going by in the opposite direction, imagining what I must have looked like the night before, right there on that freeway, drenched with tears. *Man, am I glad it was at night so no one could see me.*

I know, I know. You're betting that as soon as I saw his face, I, Marianne Loses-It Houstoun, would unexpectedly begin bawling my head off while he would wonder, "Why is she bawling her head off?" Or maybe you're thinking I, Marianne Sarcastic Houstoun, out of the blue would begin screeching, as soon as he opened the door, "SOOOOO, you don't want to MAAAARRY me, DOOOO you?"

Fortunately, neither of these scenarios occurred. As Chris opened the door for us, my usual grin appeared. "Hi," I, Marianne Act-Normal Houstoun, calmly said.

Shortly after walking in and putting our stuff down, Chris and I both agreed how nice it was to be back to normal and not all spruced up.

It was, however, still hard for me with my thoughts. Here was this man holding Cassie, making cute faces to her, while I pondered, *What's all this going to turn into? I think we're ready to get married, but if he's not, should I wait until he is? We've never talked about marriage, so do I dare start anything about it tonight or just put that thought under the rug for a little while longer?*

Between all those thoughts, I kept telling myself, *God comes first. Relax. Take a deep breath and watch that cute twenty-three-year-old man play with that cute nine-month-old girl.* Getting back to normality in thinking was slowly happening, but with new, cautioned thoughts tagging right along.

Cassie, used to her sleeping pattern, made it obvious she was tired and ready to go night-night. She fell asleep right there on that small couch in that small room in that small basement. And it's not like he had two plush chairs for us to kick back on. Nope. Remember, he was a young college student just taking care of his own self. That one chair was all he needed. We both wound up sitting on the hardwood floor talking, while Cassie continued staying cute and cozy, crashed on the couch.

Maybe if I just said the right thing, we'd then start talking about how serious our relationship is. Like they do in the movies.

Now don't get me wrong. It's not like we only talk about the weather. Quite often we shared our individual hardships. He in college, living on his own, attending classes and working. Me caring for Cassie (at two in the morning), financial thoughts for what lies ahead, and my parents' marital problems. That night was one of those nights, and then a spiritual conversation started. Another true blessing of being with a fellow believer.

I don't remember exactly what was said in that conversation, but whatever it was gave me a green light to talk to him about our relationship. *Okay, I'm ready. I can do it. Here I go. Come on, Marianne, now!*

But right then that serious topic we were discussing began to change a hair. Okay, a lot. I'll just give you a clue and say it turned into a more relaxed and romantic topic. After all, Cassie was sleeping.

That first kiss we shared six months earlier, because of that unforgettable box of homemade cookies, wasn't the only time. Kissing hello and goodbye had soon become the norm, and, as most people can understand, after months of being an official couple, kissing was downright impossible to avoid. But we knew it was best to hold off on other things, both aware of what that could lead to. From the start, we fully agreed that sex was meant for husband and wife and that it had to be avoided. We knew that the more heated we would get, the harder it would be to stop. Having learned the hard way a little over a year earlier helped me—even though difficult—keep that distance.

Maybe it was his cozy little place, with us all warm and snug on that un-romantic hardwood floor, that caused all those thoughts I had for so many hours before to fly ten thousand miles away. Gazing back and forth to one another, he said, "Honey, I... I can't wait any longer. Will you marry me?"

To this very day I will never forget how I felt. It was like I had heard the most unexpected, most romantic, and most important question in the world.

HE ASKED ME! HE ASKED ME! Oh, I couldn't care less that he didn't ask last night. HE ASKED!

"Yes. Oh, yes. I will."

"I've been wanting to ask you for a long time, and even wanted to ask you with a poem, but..."

A poem? Yep, he wanted to ask me with a poem. That's much better than making a toast at his work's dinner that he didn't do the night before. I didn't think being that happy was possible, but I learned right then I was wrong. I love being wrong.

"...but I just couldn't wait," he continued. "You see, I hadn't finished the poem yet. All last night while we were together I was thinking of asking you, [See, I was right!] but thought I should still try to finish the poem and that maybe today I could. But, as you obviously now know, I didn't. I decided there is no rule that says I *have* to give a poem."

Hearing he was not able to wait any longer to ask meant more to me than him trying to finish his poem. Needless to say, we probably had the longest kiss in the world right then, followed with more talking about our love for one another.

God must've been quietly clapping His hands, thinking, "There, second task done. My plan worked out perfectly. Marianne finally learned last night she needed Me more than Chris. Mission accomplished."

The difference between my drive home that night and my drive home the night before was like night and day. Wearing a fancy dress and high heels while drenched with rain and tears one night versus wearing jeans and tennis shoes, no rain, and grinning ear to ear the next.

I'll never forget, though, what stood out the most on my way home, something that has not once left my mind, even to this day. God wanted me to see my need for Him more than my need for anyone else. God wanted me to come to the conclusion that He needed to be first in my heart, soul, and mind. Not Chris, not Cassie, not a wedding ring, but Him. Sort of like He said, "Marianne, seek first *My* kingdom and *My* righteousness. Not Chris's. Once you realize you need to follow Me first and My plans, then look out! That hope to marry Chris shall be added unto you." That I-love-you feeling I had sensed from Jesus the night He saved me a few years earlier I was now feeling again.

I don't think anyone could have found a happier Marianne Engaged Houstoun than that pillow of hers that her head went down onto that night. That sure was me. All perfectly cozy in my perfect bed, with my perfect pillow that, as you can see, had gone through so much with me. My perfect baby lying in her perfect crib, who would soon have a perfect daddy. That room couldn't have been more, well, perfect.

Thus far you know what it had been like for me and the thoughts my pillow had soaked up as this relationship was forming. But what thoughts were filling Chris's pillow? From the beginning, as mentioned before, he wasn't looking to start a relationship with anyone. So him getting to know me didn't have, as it did for me, a goal from the start. He was just slowly getting to know some young lady while she was pregnant, and that young lady just so happened to be me. Slowly but surely, as months went by, he wasn't just falling in love with me, but falling in love with me and Cassie. No big warning was standing out (except maybe my mom asking too many flower questions), so no real red light in his mind at all. Of course *his* pillow knew his many questions of if I was THE one for him, but all men do that. God gave more pros than cons to him during those months. I'm sure his pillow and mine would have loved texting back and forth about all the thoughts Chris and I were having. And I'm sure 'LOL' would have been sent back and forth quite often.

CHAPTER 19
Woohoo!

Remember that day Chris and I went to Lamonts? You know, that store we walked into where all those rings were yelling, 'Get married. Get married. Get married'? Yeah, that store. Well, guess what? A day or two after he asked me to marry him, we went back to that store, holding hands, huge grins on our faces while walking in, staring at all those rings. How comfortable we were that time listening to all those rings hollering, 'Get married!' and we greeted every one of them as we looked. Turns out, though, that we didn't find the perfect rings there. We wound up going to another place, but I'll never forget Lamonts. That building is no longer there, but nonetheless, every time I drive by that spot, I picture that table filled with talking engagement rings.

Chris came over the day after he proposed, and boy, my parents received the title 'Happiest Parents Around.' They'd had ample opportunity to get to know him and could tell he was the one for me. Or, should I say, me *and* Cassie.

Soon after he came in and received hugs and handshakes from my parents, we walked to the phone that was connected to the kitchen wall to call his parents and tell them the good news.

"Here," Chris said, "I'll take the phone first to tell them, then I'll pass it over to you."

We both were so excited to share our good news. So there I was, watching him dial, knowing I'd most likely hear only one side of the conversation. But then again, I knew I'd hear tons of 'Woohoos' and 'Yippies' through the phone.

Ring, ring. Ring, ring.

Silence. (The person answering on the other end.)

"Hi, Dad. It's me, Chris."

Silence. (Assuming the other end said "Oh, hi, Chris. What's up?")

"Well, Dad, I couldn't wait to call you and Mom to tell you that Marianne and I are now engaged!" Chris said with the most joy-filled look on his face.

That's when I was ready to hear "YIPPIE!" or "WOOHOO!"

Silence. *Oh. They must just be smiling so much that no voices can come out. That's it.* I stared at Chris's face, assuming it would reflect their encouraging response. And it did reflect something, but not quite what I expected: a serious look.

"Yes, Dad. I do know what I'm doing."

My ear-to-ear smile turned upside down.

"What's wrong?" I whispered. *Aren't they happy with me and you?* I shuffled around Chris as their conversation went on, wishing I could shoot that phone cord, as it was obviously in the way.

Twenty thousand thoughts went everywhere.

Did we call at a bad time? Did they misunderstand him? They must not like thinking of Chris being a dad. Or ME! Am I far from being the type they want him to marry? Did they think I was weird the day we went to their house? What is it?

"Dad, I know you only met her once and I can understand why you feel this way, but believe me, I know I love her and want to marry her."

Soon his mom was on the phone, and Chris basically repeated what he had told his dad.

"Here, Mom. I'll get her now," and then covered up the phone and quietly told me, "Don't worry, honey. They just feel that they don't know you much and just... well, here. She wants to talk to you," and handed me the phone.

Instant discomfort.

Before we called I thought if I talked to her, she'd say things like, "Oh, Marianne, congratulations! I'm so at peace knowing who my son is marrying." And then I'd say stuff like "I know! Isn't it all great? I melted when he asked me!" or something along those lines. But instead she said, "I'm sure you can understand why his dad and I reacted this way and not as excited as you two thought we'd be."

"I understand." *Sort of.*

Thankfully, her last words were positive. Something like, "We look forward to getting to know you better."

Chris said a few last things to them before saying goodbye. Then, after hanging up that stupid phone with that stupid cord, he wrapped his arms around me.

"I'm sorry. Don't worry," he said reassuringly. As we talked, we both agreed on reasons why they might feel as they did and understood why they didn't light fireworks and holler hip-hip-hooraaaaaayyyyy. I mean, how would you act if you met your son's girlfriend, a twenty-year-old single mother of a nine-month-old, who had no job, no career, still living with her parents, only one time before being told they planned to get married?

I felt better as that day went by. Chris and I talked more, realizing that God's hands were even in that talk on the phone. No change of heart about getting married, that's for sure. But still, nothing could have been better for me that night than—after Chris left, with darkness in my room, Cassie zonked—me away from reality on my pillow. That pillow was hearing all my thoughts.

But I'm a good person! Their son loves me and he's a wonderful guy. We know what we're doing. Am I good enough? Maybe they're right. Maybe they should worry, 'cause maybe I am odd in some ways that I don't know about. I really did enjoy meeting them. They acted as if they really liked Cassie too. Oh, I hope I fall asleep soon.

A messy pile of thoughts on that pillow. Thankfully it ended with an eagerness to try my best to impress his parents as much as possible; to be a daughter-in-law they could be proud of, one they, eventually, couldn't imagine not having. I have to admit, though, I did feel a bit of worry thinking how that negative in-law relationship, the kind that jokingly is assumed between all mothers – and daughters-in-law, just might be proven here. Oh, great.

Letting people at church know was, yes, a totally different story. All the *yays* and *woohoos* and, of course, *finallys*, easily made up for those silent spots when telling his parents. True joy, indeed, among all. I believe Pastor Mark had the biggest smile. More peace when he'd ask "Do you, Marianne, take Chris to be your husband?" We won't talk about who else's name he came close to saying a few months prior. No, he'd be much more at peace performing this wedding.

But what was heard most at church when telling everyone was one word. "When?" I'll give you a clue. My dream of when and how long to be engaged: in June, after a six-month engagement until 'I do' would be heard, in the same place I realized love at first sight really did exist. Keep in mind, Chris was still going to college, so that was the reason behind waiting six months. We didn't want to wait any longer than we had to, so knowing his last test day was a Thursday, we both felt that having our wedding that next Saturday was soon, but waiting a whole extra week was out of the question. So we decided on getting married the Sunday after his last test day, a few hours after the church service was over. Everyone agreed that it sounded great. WOOOHOOO!

CHAPTER 20
Last Day as a Houstoun

Perfect time, right now, to share not only what I wrote in my own personal journal but also a letter I wrote to Chris.

December 12, 1987

Dear Chris,

Well, honey, it's almost one week since you asked me to marry you. Very precious, too, I might add. I just wanted to let you know what a wonderful first week it's been. Those four little words are so life changing. Chris, I'll never, ever forget the way you asked me. Holding me so very close, looking so very intently into my eyes.

I guess what has been going through my mind these first few days is how the past eight months or so have all been one big dream coming true. I remember being quite interested in you from afar. Then talking, then we started to do things after church with others, then by ourselves, then phone calls were introduced into this fast-growing relationship. Then look! What have we here? Meeting somewhere NOT on Wednesday or Sunday! Who would've thought that this same person would be, as I had prayed, the only person I would say 'I love you' to that I really meant it?

Now I look at you and think back to all those changes leading up to where we are now. I can't believe the work God has done in our lives and how He's guided us quickly into the life He has for us. I guess I want to say that when I look at you now, it's still like that first time I saw you that one day at church.

That's what most of the letter was, but before this one, I had written him so many other sweet notes, cards, and letters.

And Cassie's journal

December 18, 1987

Well, it's one week until Cassie's first Christmas. The first time she saw a tree was rather sweet. She was upstairs crying her eyes out, refusing to admit she needed a nap. I went up and got her, brought her downstairs, and when we turned around the corner and she saw the tree all lit up, she became silent.

Soon I'm sure she'll be walking. She can stand alone for quite a few seconds until she surprises herself, then falls. No teeth yet.

It's been fun wrapping her first Christmas gifts and playing the role of Santa. The best present for her, though, is not from me but from the Lord. Cassie will be getting a daddy. Chris Petersen asked me to marry him just two short weeks ago. Praise the Lord. He truly takes care of those who love Him. Needless to say, it's been MY favorite Christmas too.

Cassie, well... um, fell down the stairs. I was in our room when I heard a thud, followed by waahh, waahh, thud, thud, waahh, waahh! Thankfully she wasn't hurt, just frightened. Something like that makes me see a

*glimpse of what it would be like if she were to really
get hurt or if the Lord decided to take her from me.*

Okay, call me crazy, but what's wrong with starting another
journal? Now sure, I did have one for me and one for Cassie,
but something about having another little part of my engagement
dream coming true made me feel like I needed one more. The first
day of it will explain why.

> January 2, 1988
>
> *Why begin? How to begin? Why now to begin? What
> am I beginning anyway? Being almost a month into
> my marriage engagement to THE most wonderful man
> alive, I've realized that being engaged is something
> very special, aside from everything else before or after
> this time. The courting or dating is, in a sense, over,
> but our marriage is not yet underway. Praying that
> this will be the only time I will be in the engaged part
> of my life, I want to cherish and enjoy every part of
> it. I guess the reason for writing this will be to look
> back on my feelings about everything involved. All the
> wedding plans, all the emotions that go with this time,
> and, most importantly, how God is bringing Chris and
> me closer together and closer to Him.*

Month after month went by, some fast, some slow. His last few
college classes began to take over as the wedding date got closer,
but thankfully we had joyful interruptions like finding our first
home. Laurelwood Garden Apartments became available about
one month before the wedding, so we were able to move a few
things in. Unforgettable.

> April 14
>
> *I'm totally thrilled for so many reasons, but mostly
> because I can now easily picture our little family unit
> since I know where we'll be living. The anxiety of*

finding a place is no longer on my mind. The money worries are so much less too. Praise God again and again. Now my efforts in getting stuff together can be done with more anticipation. Cassie has the chickenpox. Poor girl.

I could share lots of little things that went on during those six months, like about us looking through tons of wedding invitation samples. "So, honey, out of all those we've looked at, which one do you think is the best?" Turned out we liked the same one!

I could also write how thankful I was for his parents. The more time I got to spend with them, the more I could tell, again, God was spoiling me. But what I must share is that Cassie began to warm up to Chris as more time went by. It wasn't long before she would say hi to him as soon as she saw him. Natural warmth grew. The stamp of 'Dad' was showing on his heart, too, as each month passed.

But like I said, his classes were draining. It wasn't unheard of to have an entire week go by without seeing him. I was getting to see a side of him that made me think, just a hair, he wasn't perfect anymore. *Hard to believe, but I think I'm beginning to see a wee bit of a flaw in him.*

Engagement Journal

> May 18, 1988
> *Chris was a bit down tonight. I'm sure being behind in school really gets his mind out of sorts, making him a time or two (or three) simply keeping to himself. I pray I could just swallow my selfishness and not let Chris feel like he needs to watch Cassie as much. Sometimes he needs to, but other times I need to let him be away from her, too. I ache seeing Chris do all he does by himself. I wish I could kidnap him, take him away, and make him forget all his worries.*

May 20, 1988

Real quick, before I go to sleep, I dislike Chris's classes very, very much. This journal is one of the few outlets I can turn to to get out some of my feelings that aren't good for me to unload on Chris. I try so hard to understand his school load, and I do, but it's still hard. I see him less and less, and when I think to myself all day "tonight I'll get to see him," and then I don't, my emotions are robbed and it's very difficult to keep a cheery attitude. I lift my thoughts up to you, Lord, so I can get some sleep.

June 3, 1988

The wedding is now only nine days away, but oh, what an insensitive twit I feel I am so much of the time. Chris is beating his brains out finishing all the schoolwork he needs to get done, plus his job, and the private thoughts I've had these last few days have been so selfish. I pray none of my thoughts are being conveyed by my actions and attitude.

Yes, the wedding was almost a week ahead at this point. We all know how busy planning a wedding can be nowadays, and wedding planning has even become a career for many. Not so much, however, in the late eighties. In comparison, our wedding planning stayed very simple. Not easy as pie, mind you, but compared to a majority today, it was a piece of cake. His parents were so helpful in it as well, and my dear mom gave it her all. By this point we had gotten all our things needed in the apartment, and Chris was actually living there. Yep, all was set.

Like I said, the wedding was to be at our church, followed by the reception at my parents' home, weather permitting, in the big, spacious backyard. My mom was rarin' to deal with most of the food as well, with, thankfully, some help.

Dealing with all the wedding plans took up about sixty-five percent of my time that last week. Sad to say, it felt like only fifteen percent was given to Cassie, but that smile she still gave me was surely needed. Naps had never been more appreciated. So, twenty percent left. Chris got fifteen percent of that. Gold, yes, but so little. Studying for tests was all he could think about, because studying was on his mind *all* the time. Seemed that way to me, anyway.

So now five percent left. That five percent was me on my pillow. My thoughts were tired that last week. Oh, sure, the wedding would somehow happen. A few relatives would be in town soon. By now it seemed everything inside or outside the house had something to do with the reception. But in my room at night, with Cassie sleeping, my pillow and I were in our own little world. No decorations, no wrapping paper, no flowers, no balloons, no list to check off, no table decor. And, best of all, no light. Just me, all covered up under my blankets and cut off from the world, on my pillow. My thoughts were filled with joy, yes, but still concerns and questions. After all, Chris hadn't been the most adorable man as of late. And I knew I'd be doing lots of adjusting in the days and weeks and months to come.

Do I really want to share Cassie every day? It's not going to be easy having someone else as head of the house. And I really did love having my own little world at the end of each day, in my own room and on my own cozy bed night after night. But, once married, it wouldn't only be me, myself, and I, and Cassie.

I so wish Chris could have shown more excitement this last week or two. But no. His classes, along with his normal hours at work, have been the boss. My pillow heard all my thoughts. *Why? Why? Why can't he just show a bit more love to me instead of to those books and work?*

I know there's always stress involved with wedding planning, but taking care of my fifteen-month-old sure didn't help, along with me forcing myself not to come across stressed, for Chris's sake. I knew he felt bad not helping, and I didn't want to make him feel worse. God heard me plead over and over again, night after night, for strength to keep on keeping on.

June 3, 1988
I need to keep in mind Jesus and His attitude and His selflessness. He sacrificed so much for me. I need to learn the art of sacrifice. I pray I may learn from my sour attitude inside and use it to grow and to become a better wife to Chris. I love him so much. God's will is perfect; His ways are perfect; His motives are perfect. Praise the Lord!

Each morning that week I woke up knowing the countdown continued. My last Monday as a Houstoun. My last Tuesday as a Houstoun. The list of what still needed to be done was getting smaller. The joy of knowing I'd finally be marrying my first love was getting bigger. My last Wednesday as a Houstoun.

I hadn't seen Chris at all since the Sunday before. His final week of classes was pretty much tests, so the last hours of studying for them took over. That, along with his normal job. Not easy for me, that's for sure.

But then, finally, my last Thursday as a Houstoun. However, I got to happily add one more title to that day: Chris's last testing day! His last day at school, thus no more ignoring his fiancée whom he's marrying in three days! I loved that fact.

The plan of attack for that day at home was major. By this point Cassie loved walking, almost too well for a busy mom who was needing to go everywhere to do everything. No more simply tossing her in a crib with a bottle while getting things done. Having Willma and Eyde around, plus my sister Kelly, helped big time, and they enjoyed watching her while I took care of wedding-prep necessities.

So much to think about that Thursday, but my main thought the entire day was filled with worry. No, not worrying if going to a totally new hairstylist two hours before the wedding was wise. No, not worrying if having my sister sing a song during the wedding while my soon-to-be brother-in-law played the piano would be flawless. And no, not even worrying how the weather would be, hoping the reception could be in the backyard. Okay, maybe a little worrying about that, but nothing compared to the worry of Chris's plans.

Was this man I was to marry in three days going to come to the house that evening? He'd probably rather go crash at the apartment since, after those stinking tests, he still had to go to work. I'm sure he's fried. And even if he did come here like he said he would, he'd be too frazzled to really gaze into my eyes. I'm sure if he did come, he'd be crashed on the couch in two minutes.

A few more hours went by. *Okay, future wifey-poo. Assume the worst, but hope for the best. He's tired, more tired than ever. Just be glad he's done and assume he still wants to get married on Sunday. I hope he can remember what it is about me that makes him want to live with me for the rest of his life.*

I can picture it now. The sun was on its way down on that beautifully warm summer evening. My mom and I were right outside the spacious three-car garage, having just put a few more reception needs inside. We were about to call it a night, both thinking Chris would have been there by then. Just as I was about to click the electric garage door to come down, assuming he wasn't going to make it, Mom and I both noticed his car pulling up the driveway.

"I think I'll go inside now," my ever-so-wise mother said. "I'll let you close the door."

HE'S HERE! Happiness. *Better late than never, but what's he gonna be like? That's the question.* I was ready to see an exhausted man slowly get out and grab a few things before walking over, hearing something like, "Hi, honey. I'm so tired. I'm sorry, but do you mind if I go crash in the TV room?" But no. What I saw was far from that. He parked, got out, and with no delay, came right over to me.

"Oh, honey, I'm so sorry I'm getting here later than planned. Knowing I'll be away from work for a week, I had to finish a few things." The look on his face was nothing like what I had expected. He was wide awake.

Having put his hands on my shoulders just as that gorgeous sun began to disappear, he looked straight into my eyes and continued, "Marianne, all day I've been wanting to tell you how sorry I am for how it's been this last month. I know I've been in my own world because of the classes."

He's looking straight into my eyes. Keep talking. Keep talking. "All that studying, plus still going to work. I'm so sorry for not giving you the attention you deserve. But I am back. I love you and I cannot wait till our wedding. Please believe me when I say I'm so excited and so ready to help these last few days. I love you."

Wait. Is this the same man who's been in outer space lately? That man whose ears have been closed while his eyes have been glued to books and notes? The man I knew I loved but lately haven't really, well... liked? Yes, that same gorgeous man I fell in love with from the first time I saw him was back.

That night we didn't do one speck of wedding preparation. Heck, we knew the next few days would be filled with all those activities. That night we simply enjoyed getting used to not thinking of anything else but each other. Since he was, at this point, staying in our future apartment that wasn't too far away, he eventually went there that night. I bet as soon as he got in, he went straight to bed, falling asleep before his head even hit his pillow.

And one thing's for sure, that night my pillow could sense a new me. No questions about Chris and whether he was still perfect for me or if he still loved me could be found. My practical wedding-planning thoughts got pushed under the rug for a spell as well. My pillow probably thought, "Oh, great. Back to all those ooey-gooey, lovey-dovey thoughts."

Friday had arrived. After one of the best night's sleep he'd had in a long time, Chris came back to the house. As soon as he showed up and gave a sweet hug to Cassie, my mom and I updated him with all that had been done and what was left to do. I hadn't dared to inform him much about it all these last few weeks, but now he knew. He also got to meet a few relatives who had flown in.

The only work I remember that he and I did that day was blowing up tons of balloons to make one huge heart-shaped design to put on the back outside wall of the house for the reception. We were just kicking back, outside in the sun, blowing up and tying the balloons, while sharing little this-and-that's about whatever came up. I could tell he was enjoying not having to think of a test or projects from work. Of course, a few flirtatious comments were passed back and forth. All he and I needed to deal with was who could blow up and then tie the balloons the fastest.

We did do other things that day as well, like discuss all the who, what, where, when, and how questions for the wedding day and honeymoon. We knew, though, it was best to keep the why of the wedding as the foundation of it all. Things got done fairly smoothly. Now, if you asked my mom if she felt it was going smoothly, she might have had a different answer.

My last Saturday as a Houstoun had arrived. Wait! It wasn't only my last Saturday as a Houstoun, but my last full *day* as a Houstoun. No more waking up on a Saturday morning needing to think only of me, myself, and I. Oh, and of course, my one and only Cassie. My last night, for the most part, all to myself. Me and my pillow, the last night in our own little world. No more going to bed on my own, not needing to care who else was around. I didn't ponder on that idea too much, though. Knowing I was soon to marry my Mr. Right easily covered that self-filled thought.

I'm sure if I hadn't waited twenty-nine years since our wedding day to write this book, I would have remembered a bit more of what took place on that day. For sure, though, I can picture tons of decor lying around on the kitchen table. Visiting relatives did all they could to help, either by doing what they were told or just by getting out of the way. Of course my mom was the busiest.

Kind of weird, but the only part of that day I don't remember much of was the rehearsal. I do remember laughing at the pretend wedding vows Pastor Mark had us repeat. Not so much the words themselves, but all the laughter they caused. But that's really about it.

What I do remember, though, is the after-rehearsal dinner. No big fancy whoop-di-do restaurant, but one sweet and simple place in Burien called Shakey's Pizza. Nice and cozy for about twenty hungry folks, all relaxing and enjoying the reason we were together. I'm sure if we had cell phones then, tons of selfies would have been taken. But instead, those oldie-but-goodie pics were being taken which, if you remember, took days to get developed.

Most Saturday nights prior to this one, Chris and my last words were always the same. "Goodnight. See ya at church tomorrow." That night, however, those same words were said but just a little bit differently. How? With a bit more of an eloquent, meaningful sound. And why? We both knew that was the last time those words would be said.

CHAPTER 21
Dreams Come True

The night finally arrived. My last night as a Houstoun, getting Cassie and myself ready for bed in my room. "Goodnight, Cass," I said while putting her down. It wasn't Cassie's last night in that room. My mom would be putting her to bed there for four more nights while Chris and I would be on our honeymoon. That night, however, was *my* last time putting her to bed in our mommy-daughter bedroom. Sort of a weird feeling. No more nights in the room I grew up in. My last night there as Marianne Still-Single Houstoun. My room was soon to become the next guest room. I just avoided that thought and went back downstairs as soon as Cassie was all calm and cozy.

"So, is my Winnipoops ready for tomorrow?" Dad asked, ready to retire for the night. I knew I wouldn't have much time to chat with him in the morning, so we talked a few minutes more before calling it a night.

Now, it wasn't just mornings my mom was by that fireplace, but most evenings as well, with the one difference being that some nights it wasn't coffee but wine. I'll tell you one thing, that was for sure a wine night after all the hustle and bustle she'd done that day.

My last night in that house as a Houstoun. My last time sitting on that couch as a Houstoun. And knowing the next day would be just a hair abnormal, that night might've been my last time talking with my mom, just she and I by that fireplace, one

Houstoun to another. All the business of the day was over and we were enveloped in silence.

I know I must have thanked my mom at least half a million times for all she'd done before that night, but that night, I said thank you for the other half a million. So nice. Calm. Quiet. Perhaps a few last thoughts on Cassie's care and reception details, but not much. We had done enough. "Well, Mom, time I go crash. And Mom, thanks again."

Years of so many thoughts were soaking on my pillow that night. I bet that pillow did some reminiscing, as well, on how many tears and smiles it witnessed through all the trials, sorrows, and joys it had felt over those years. From me wishing my sister Kelly—as we shared the same room for years—would have let me play the music I wanted in our room, to that ever-so-joyful jumping on my bed that first day that the room was all mine. The many sad times at night feeling overweight, or thinking about problems between my parents, or crazy things my siblings had done, or how cool I felt having senior friends, Willma and Eyde, my freshman year at Highline High School.

My main thought on that last night on that pillow as a Houstoun, all alone, was how just over a year before, God had lifted me up out of the most confusing, anxious, uncertain, and discouraging time of my life and held me with as much care as a father would hold his own child. He had my pregnancy go smoothly while guiding me in His perfect direction, all the while knowing that He was going to gently put me down in the arms of the man He knew was best for me. And I still picture that, twenty-nine years later.

Somehow I did manage to fall asleep that night, because before I knew it, I woke up. Sunday morning. June 12, 1988. Not your normal getting-ready-for-church morning, *that's* for sure. I know if I had written this book weeks after the wedding, I'd remember more of what I did that morning, but it's 2018 now, so the details are a bit foggy. I just recall how abnormal I felt. Abnormal driving myself to church for the last time from my Normandy Park home.

Abnormal going to a normal church service, knowing it wasn't going to really feel normal. Abnormal taking my, I repeat, *my* daughter into the nursery, knowing the next Sunday Cassie's *dad* might take her. Abnormal finally seeing Chris that morning, the man I was to marry that afternoon. But all those abnormal feelings melted away in the blink of an eye. *There he is. Soon to be all mine.*

We both showed a different type of smile when we walked toward one another. And all the people there just grinned, sensing, too, that the aroma in the air that morning was a bit different.

Okay, I'll be honest. There wasn't much from the sermon message I was able to focus on or remember except, well, the last word of that last prayer: amen. I'm sure you can understand why, but if by chance you don't, I was about to say 'I do' to the man sitting right next to me in about four hours, that's why.

Normally, after the service most people just chit-chatted while their kids wandered around. But not that day. Nope. People either began setting things up for the wedding or just took off, knowing they'd soon be back.

All I could really think about by that point were three things. First and by far the most precious, how I'd get to say 'I do' very soon to that man standing right next to me. Second, how glad I was I did not have to do any church prep work. And third, MY HAIR!! *I have to leave sooner than the rest. My hair is waiting. OH, it had better turn out good! I have to go now. Come on, Chris, let's go. Let's go!*

Chris and I, a lot sooner than normal, began walking out as most others said things like, "So sweet knowing we'll all be back soon for your wedding" or "One special Lord's day, indeed." And one dear couple, pretty much the same age as us, took us away from the others and gave us a few—how shall I word it?—humorous newlywed gifts. Boy, there was some good chuckling going on as Chris and I unwrapped them. Waving goodbye began taking place as we got closer to our cars.

That was the first Sunday in quite some time we didn't all three get in his car and drive to my parents' home, planning to come back later for the evening service. It felt a bit strange that he'd get in his car, I'd get in mine, and we'd go our separate ways. *His last time seeing me before I walk down the aisle. Our last kiss before our first kiss as husband and wife.* Yes, we wanted the traditional waiting till I walk down the aisle to see one another.

All calm and collected, I waved to a few people as I nonchalantly pulled out of the parking lot. However, one block later, WHAM! My carefree, relaxed-looking face did a U-turn as if there were a sign that popped out of my car that read 'EEK! 'I DO' IN THREE HOURS!'

"Here, Kelly. Here's Cassie's lunch. Her nap's right after that," was the first of the twenty million things I said as I came into the house.

"Where's my stuff? Oh, there it is." Rush, rush. "Mom, make sure Dad's ready when I get back from getting my hair done. Kelly, you're sure you have all of Cassie's clothes and stuff?"

"Marianne, we have it all taken care of," someone said as I headed out the door to get my hair beautified.

For some crazy reason, I still remember what it was like in that hair place. You know, one of those places you think of every time you drive by even years later. Thankfully I was the only one there. My head lying back, hair in the sink.

I must have said "I'm getting married" fifteen different ways to that lady. She tried a few different looks with my hair as I looked back and forth from my watch to the mirror and back to my watch. Finally, "That's it!" *Yippie, yippie, yippie. She's done!* After paying, including a nice tip, I jumped back in the car. *Wait. This is the very last time I'm driving this car. After today, it's just Mom and Dad's. How sad.* The car I did all those important drives in, going to and from California, and then to the Crisis Pregnancy Center where I got my pregnancy test, those two trips to the airport, picking up Greg and dropping him back off, and those two evenings in a row driving out to see Chris, all took place in my parents' four-door sedan. The plan now was for Chris and me to use his car until one more could be added. So all those years of using that car had come to an end. Sort of sad. But you know what? That thought didn't last long as soon as I pulled up the driveway.

Walking in, I saw how most everything was all set up for the reception. I saw Mom, Dad, Kelly, along with my brother David. The ladies there gave the appropriate ooohs and aaahs over my hair. My dad was the only one ready to go, being that he was going to take me to church as soon as I got home.

I quickly grabbed all I needed to take.

Dress – check (and yes, a dream dress)

Shoes – check

Makeup – check

All needs for the, um... wedding night – check

I knew we'd be coming back to the house the next day before taking off for our four-night honeymoon, so it was nice not needing to pack everything for that before the wedding.

"Okay, Dad, I think I'm all ready. Let's go," I said while holding Cassie one last time before leaving.

"Don't worry about Cassie, Marianne," my sisters and mom took turns saying. "We'll all make sure she'll be adorable. Now GO!"

My last time in any car as a Houstoun was with Mr. Houstoun himself. It had been eons since I had been in a car with Dad. Guess what we talked about? Remember the title of that one book, *Men Are From Mars, Women Are From Venus*? Well, it's true. What he brought up on that sweet ten-minute drive was about, drumroll please, a certain car problem and how it can get fixed. Don't ask. I just sort of rolled my eyes and said "oh, really?" in the perfect tone at the appropriate times.

We're there. The church has two buildings. One was the main church-service building and the other, next to it with about ten yards distance between, was the children's nursery building.

"Okay, Dad, I'm going in that one building there to get ready.

We call it the nursery building," I said, relieved to be done talking about car repairs. "The wedding will be in that other building. You could just stay in the car until others you know show up, which should be really soon."

"Sounds good," and then he ended with the sweetest words. "Winnipoops, I'm so happy for you. I love you." That made up for all that auto-fixing advice he gave during my last car ride as a Houstoun.

If you've ever been to a wedding, then you know how it all looks an hour or so before the renown 'I now pronounce you' is heard. That also means I don't need to get into much detail about us ladies chit-chatting away about makeup, hairstyles, and whatnot. With Willma as the maid of honor, Eyde and my sister Janis as the bridesmaids, I savored it all.

I can't really give Chris's side of getting ready for the wedding 'cause, well, I wasn't there. I just know time flew by fast. The best part about getting ready was when the last clip-this, tie-that, and pin-those were done. Right about then was when my sister Kelly brought Cassie in.

Another unforgettable moment, seeing my fifteen-month-old daughter right then and there. Life stopped. Everything, to me, went silent. I couldn't really just drop my bouquet and pick her up and squeeze her to pieces while spinning around. Instead, I slowly knelt down enough to put my arms around her. Her hair was still very short, so I was glad her pink dress clarified she was my precious little daughter. It was as if all the engrossed thoughts of getting ready for the wedding were thrown under the rug. Me and my daughter, soon to be Mrs. and Miss Petersen.

Cassie had a bit of an odd look on her face because of all that was going on around her. And, as soon as she saw me, she was probably wondering, "Mom, why in the *world* do you look so weird?"

But reality did hit when my sister spoke up. "It's best I take her now to go find a seat." And off they went.

All guests were sitting. It's time. Everyone's in place. Let the wedding begin.

Everyone who'd been getting ready for the wedding stepped out of the nursery building and headed to that other door. All except me, Miss Marianne About-To-Say-I-Do Houstoun. I stayed inside, knowing it would still be a few minutes until I would need to leave. Dad stood between both buildings, along with the others in the wedding party.

I was all on my own in the nursery. All by myself. That is, of course, with my Engagement Journal.

> June 12, 1988
>
> *Well, a few more minutes to go!! I'm all dressed (whew) and have enough time to collect my frame of mind. It's been so stressful, yet so worth it. It's nice to know that God is in control of all things, even spark-plug problems. UGH! I'm all ready and I hope Chris is pleasantly surprised.*

I had intended to write more, but I do believe I got the time-to-walk-out look from my dad, with his right arm making the come-over-here, come-over-here move. I put my journal down. All done. I'm sure if there had been more time, I would have ended it with this:

Thank you, God, for allowing my wedding dreams to come true.
1 – I am marrying the first man I truly fell in love with
2 – I'm wearing that perfect wedding dress
3 – My best friend is my maid-of-honor
4 – We are getting married during the summer
5 – We had a six-month engagement
6 – We're waiting till our wedding night
Heck, even an extra secret wish was able to fit in:
7 – We both don't like coffee.

I bet I would have also ended it with my favorite verse, Matthew

6:33: 'Seek first the kingdom of God and His righteousness, and all these things'—like marrying the man I've always dreamed of—'shall be added unto you.' (I couldn't help but add a few of my own words in that verse.)

My dad and I met between buildings. We slowly walked arm in arm those ten yards or so to the main entrance. (Believe it or not, he shared one last little car fact with me on the way over. And you know what? I smile whenever I think of that.)

The pianist begins. Time for my dad to escort me down the aisle. I see Chris; Chris sees me. I melt. My wedding dream is in full action.

A few unforgettable parts of that wedding. Kelly's song came out just beautifully as my soon-to-be brother-in-law played the piano. Chris's own father, my future father-in-law, whose job at the time was a chaplain, gave a few perfect, encouraging words during the wedding as well. And how dare I forget when Kelly's son Danny, about three years old, walked down the middle aisle during the ceremony. Best of all, and most important, however, was when our dear Pastor Mark asked those two most important questions. "Do you, Chris, take Marianne..." I loved those words. "And do you, Marianne, take Chris..." You bet I do. "I now pronounce you husband and wife."

I could end this story right here. I could also do the opposite and add another chapter or two to describe how everyone loved the big heart decoration at the reception made with all those balloons, or how I learned the hard way that if a bride smiles solidly for hours, her jaws can get pretty sore. I could share how we hadn't really eaten much at the reception, so grabbed a bite at a nice restaurant right after the festivities were done. Those serving us shared, "Not many brides keep their wedding dresses on anymore. Great to see you did!" and gave us great service.

Of course, I know you'd love to read how the honeymoon went. Come on, be honest.

But no, that's not how I will end this story. Instead, I want you to picture how, after we exchanged our 'I dos' and after that wonderful first kiss as husband and wife, as my bouquet was handed back to me and we turned toward the guests and looked out to everyone, and after the piano was heard and we took a few steps to begin walking out, we stopped. Right then my sister Kelly carried Cassie over to not just her mother, but to both her mother and father, Mr. and Mrs. Petersen. You see, we knew it wasn't just a new family of two that started this new chapter in life right then and there. Chris and I felt this new family of three started this new chapter, so we all walked down the rest of the way together.

I imagine God at this point pushing His recliner all the way back, hands behind His head, eyes closed while taking one deep breath, and, while slowly exhaling, thinking, "Mission accomplished."

The new Petersen Family of Three

Marianne and Cassie then   Marianne and Cassie now

Father-to-be Chris & Daughter-to-be Cassie

Mr. and Mrs. Petersen

CHAPTER 22
Conclusion

Why my story? Why share how a true, yet young, follower of Christ can mess up and fall into sin, causing a major detour on her planned freeway to success? The main reason for sharing my story is to show how God forgives one of His own who sees their sin, repents, turns away from it, and turns toward Christ.

Do you have the feeling that what you've done or gotten yourself into is wrong? What about the consequences? Are you, as I was, not able to pursue your long-term dream of a career? Is your pillow aware of how often you've cried from past or present hurts? Have you thought over and over again "Why, God?" Yes, I still felt extremely low at times with the many things going on around me, but He did enough to have me believing somehow, some way, better days were ahead.

In this day and age, with all our technology, we often wish God would text us His plans overnight. No promise of that, however. That's where the word "faith" comes in. For me, it was a snowball effect. Something happened that showed me God was there: that first unanswered phone call to Planned Parenthood. I didn't realize that instantly, but while walking back to my car after my pregnancy test, I did. Faith in God began. Slowly I was becoming Marianne Trying-to-Master-What-Faith-Means Houstoun.

Family and friends showed me much love, and the snowball got bigger. God provided a Christian doctor; my faith grew more. Sure, the reason my mom became King Kong after finding out that illegal secret melted my faith a bit. But as my pillow soaked up my thoughts and tears as months went by, perhaps it could also sense my faith slowly growing again. It was not easy, of course. After all, God did need to cause that drive at night in the rain, coming home when bawling my head off, almost literally, to have me realize I had pushed Him off to the side a bit too far. But even that was His plan; thus, perfect. God allows things to happen to strengthen us as we learn more about our faith, our faults, and just how much we need Him. God uses our trials to mold and shape us, to conform us to what He wants you and I to be. So hold on tight and remember that faith is not knowing what the future holds, but knowing Who is holding your future.

I'm not here to tell anyone what they should do. Keep the baby? Give that baby up for adoption? I was, for a short time, thinking of adoption myself. But like I said, I felt I could keep the baby. Your pregnancy may be the very means God uses to bless a childless couple. There are millions of women who often cry themselves to sleep on their own pillows, wishing they could have a baby. Perhaps God wants to use you to make their wish come true. Whatever your thoughts, pray for His help in making one of the most important decisions you will ever make.

There are many people and organizations who guide many going through this seemingly impossible road. Here are a few to give you a taste of what kinds of help is available.

– optionline.org
– pregnancydecisionline.org
– unplannedpregnancy.com

Before I bring my story to a close, I can't help but share a few last things.
First; some verses that I still cling tightly to. (New King James Version)

Isaiah 41:10

Don't be afraid, for I am with you. Don't be discouraged, for I am your God. I will strengthen you and help you. I will hold you up with my victorious right hand.

Psalm 139:14

For You formed my inward parts; You covered me in my mother's womb. I will praise You, for I am fearfully and wonderfully made.

Matthew 6:33 (my personal favorite)

But seek first the kingdom of God and His righteousness, and all these things shall be added to you.

Fact: I love music—always have, always will, so I have to tell you about a song that fit perfectly into this episode of my life: "Just Be Held," by Casting Crowns. The words describe so clearly how God lifted me up during the toughest times and held me tightly through it all. In the arms of God I was held, and He didn't let me go. As months passed, He let me know my life was not falling apart but falling into place. And even if I didn't feel like I could hold on, I could tell I was still being held.

God and My Pillow was written to bring at least one reader a measure of comfort. My sincere desire is that my story will give you hope. If that is accomplished, then my goal has been fulfilled.

Sincerely,

Marianne Loves-Her-Diamond-Studded-Hands Petersen

CLOSING

Now, God didn't just say "Ahh, what a cute family of three I enjoyed bringing together. The rest will be their own doing." No, far from it. Many extra blessings came from that day. For instance, as weeks, months, and even years went by, Chris and I loved hearing those who didn't know the story say something like, "She looks just like her dad." Chris and I just smiled, with an occasional wink to one another. What's cool is that they were right: she did!

After about a year, legal paperwork was completed, having obtained Greg's signature allowing Chris to become Cassie's legal father. Even though it felt from day one that Cassie had her dad right there by her side, the January calendar of 1989 had the words 'Adoption Day' noticeably written for the first time, with those same two words put on the calendar year after year. A little Petersen celebration, indeed. That wedding day was the beginning of our, to this day, twenty-nine-year marriage. In all those years I didn't just keep journals for Cassie and myself, but by the time Cassie was ten, I had a total of five journals going. Do your math. Mine, Cassie's, and, yep, three more. One more daughter and two sons, in that order. The Petersen family of three had become a family of six. Seven, total, if you include the family dog.

There was a time after our second child was born, shortly after having moved into a home, I felt a desire to 'do unto others as you would have them do unto you.' Better worded, I wanted to do unto others as they DID unto me. I was so thankful God had planned for me to go to the Crisis Pregnancy Center that I wanted to volunteer there somehow, someway, and volunteered for their hotline.

Are you curious what went on with Cassie's biological father? Only a few things occurred between us after I dropped him off at the airport. No connection at all during the remaining pregnancy. After Cassie was born, I mailed a short letter to Greg including facts on size, weight, and whatnot. No request for money or other future needs was included. The letter was simple enough that I could have just texted it to him if that had been available back then. He showed no sign of expecting much, if any, information from my end, so I thought it best to keep it short. We had not said anything about keeping in contact, and I'm sure it's because we both knew it was best not to. Being young, ignorant, and a bit scared, I think we both felt we would only connect again if we had to.

The second and last connection was years later, not with Greg himself, but his mother. One evening, when the Petersen family of six was at the dinner table—Cassie was about twelve, our youngest was three, along with our two middle tykes, six and nine—the phone rang.

"Hello," answered Chris. "Yes, here she is," and handed me the cordless phone. (Notice I said cordless.)

I got up, walked over to him, and took the phone as all the kids stared at me, wondering who it was. Chris shrugged his shoulders up, obviously showing he had no idea.

"Hello, this is Marianne."

"Marianne, I hope it's okay I call. This is Greg's mom, Laura."

WHAT! Why in the world is SHE calling?

"Well, hello, Laura," I said with my own look of curiosity on my face. I then pointed to our computer room (Yes, there were computers by then!) to let my family know where I'd be.

"Marianne, you're probably wondering why I'm calling you, right?"

I was in that room, holding the phone, with an intense look of wonder on my face.

"And you're probably wondering why we made no attempt to connect with you at all after the baby, my very own granddaughter, was born."

*Um, hellooo, you sure got **that** right.*

"I'll be honest. That thought did occur a time or two," I replied.

"The reason is . . ." she said rather slowly.

Yes? Yes, tell me . . . pleeeeeease.

But during those few seconds of silence, she began to cry. Then she went on with her story. Turns out, unbeknownst to me, Greg and I almost got married at the same time his parents signed their divorce papers. At about the same time Greg returned home, she headed off to Italy, where she was originally from, to live with her parents.

"After being in Italy these last twelve years, I came back just yesterday, back to this house," she said before more tears. "As soon as I came in here, I saw this information about the adoption right here on the kitchen counter."

Turns out, having been gone those twelve years, she had heard nothing about me having the baby or about the adoption until that day she came back home.

"It was very hard for me to read this. I've thought of my grandchild every day all these years. Now, reading this, finding out it's a granddaughter I have, I had to call to see how she's doing."

I melted. "Cassie is now twelve years old and has one sister and two brothers. And my husband, Chris, is the best loving father. She is very healthy, plays piano, loves to sing," and on and on I went. I made sure she knew how healthy and happy Cassie was and how I was a stay-at-home mom who homeschooled.

More tears. She then went on to explain a bit more.

"The main reason all this is so hard is because Greg is . . ." (more crying) ". . . he's . . . he's dead."

I was stunned. "He's dead? Oh, I'm so sorry. When was this?"

"Only a few years ago. I'm sorry, but I won't get into how," (more crying) "but he's now dead."

She then shared how he, as years passed, messed with alcohol and drugs. Sad, yes, but I wasn't totally shocked. On top of it all, she said he had actually fathered another child even before meeting me! *Something ELSE he didn't tell me.*

I then started thinking perhaps he purposely overdosed on something and she was too ashamed to bring that part up. I didn't dare ask.

Another minute or two went by.

"Take good care of my granddaughter, Marianne. Thanks for talking."

I made sure I thanked her for calling as well. I'll never forget how I felt as I walked out of that room. I cherished even more that family I saw sitting around the dining room table.

"Who was that?" Chris asked.

Now keep in mind, we had told Cassie from the start about how special the adoption day was and what it was all about. And as she got older, we shared more details. So since she knew, I had no problem saying, "Well, Cassie, it was your biological father's mother." Chris and Cassie's eyes instantly opened big time. "WHAT?"

I remember Cassie walking over to me as I stood in the hallway. *I bet she's going to ask more questions about him. She'll start crying and say something about how she wished one day she could have met him. What in the world do I say?*

I told Cassie most of what his mother and I had talked about. Notice I said *most*, not all. I started telling her how her father's mother was in Italy because she and her parents came from there. I then told the rest. Not, however, the bad stuff Greg was into and my thoughts on perhaps how he died.

There, I'm done. Story's over. What's Cassie going to say? Get ready to answer twenty million questions.

"Oh, really?" she responded. "I didn't know I'm part Italian."

Cool! That was it? NO WAY! That was sure easy. I grabbed her as she started walking away, hugging her to pieces, letting her know her mommy loves her.

After that call, nothing had been brought up for years. I'm not complaining. To me, it meant that Chris was her dad and that's all that mattered.

My darling Cassie is now, as I finish this book, thirty-two years old and the one to blame for having me learn . . . I LOVE BEING A GRANDMOTHER! There, I let it out.

I'll never forget what happened while babysitting my granddaughter when she was about two months old. As I was rocking her in my arms, gazing down at her adorable face for a few seconds, it felt like I was holding Cassie when she was that little. They looked identical at that age. I literally had to shake my head. *Um, Me, that is your granddaughter, not Cassie. You're forty-two, not twenty. Shake it off.*

And now I can't hold back the rest of the blessings. Our other daughter, Trina, is also married and has two sons and two daughters. You can now call me Marianne Loves-Being-Grammom-To-five Petersen.

2020 is now upon us, and I have remained happily married for thirty-two years to that same man who proved to me that love at first sight does exist and that God just might go that extra mile, using even coffee to show you He's planned that road ahead.

ACKNOWLEDGEMENTS

As mentioned in the preface, Michelle Novak, was the final tool God used to convince me to turn my memories into print. If it wasn't for her, you would not be reading my story.

My heartfelt thanks to Lori Ann Grover, an experienced author, who connected me with the Northwest Christian Writer's Association (NCWA), that opened up the writing world for me. Starbuck talks with Sonja Anderson; the writers' critique group I was in; and Lynette Bishop, my carpool buddy to and from our monthly meetings. But most important, it was through NCWA that I found my editor, Sheryl Madden. How and when I met her got me holding even stronger to my favorite saying - God's timing is perfect. NCWA also was behind me finding Lynnette Bonner for the book cover, and Jon Stewart for every page in between. God still hears my many thanks for NCWA.

I also thank the cheerleader in my story, Willma Redhed, or better yet Willma Behind-the-Scenes-Wording-Fixer-Upper-Logo-Creator Redhed. Not sure what I would have done without meeting her years ago (even though she wore those weird shorts.)

From start to finish, my husband, Chris, the one who proved to me love at first sight is real. He has graciously allowed me hours upon hours to work on my book at home or watching me leave the house to go here and there to do this or that for my writing. And yes, we still love not drinking coffee together.

And how do I dare leave out the tool God used to show me He is there: Cassie. Thank you, Cassie, for being the best reason for me even writing this book.

Time for that saying 'Save the Best For Last': God. He gets my highest acknowledgement of thanks. From the day He opened my eyes to the fact that I was one of His, to the day this book you are reading got into your hands, He has been pulling and/or pushing me from the first page to the last. Indeed, the best help I've gotten has been from God.

Oh, and of course, my pillow.

About the Author

Marianne Petersen lives in the Seattle area with her husband. They have four children, all now adults, and five grandchildren. She is a member of the Northwest Christian Writers' Association. Marianne shares her writings on various websites, and enjoys sharing her weekly blog posts. Her second memoir is in the making, with the hope that it, too, will encourage others.

God and My Pillow has received two awards, and has been rated 5 stars by most readers.

Marianne works from home as a video editor/publisher, and she is thankful she can adjust her hours when being 'Gram-mom' is needed. She has passions for photography and music, and is an enthusiastic runner and writer. There's a part of her, though, that always wishes she had more time to just sit and read a good book.

Website/Blog:	www.mariannesmemoirs.com
Twitter:	@marimemoirs
Facebook:	@mariannesmemoirs
email:	marianne@mariannesmemoirs.com

CPSIA information can be obtained
at www.ICGtesting.com
Printed in the USA
FSHW020024170320
68122FS